SECRET BRITAIN

MARY-ANN OCHOTA

SECRET BRITAIN

UNEARTHING OUR MYSTERIOUS PAST

FRANCES
LINCOLN

Contents

Introduction

Every step you take in Britain treads on the past. A street now filled with shops and houses might once have been a royal palace. An anonymous farmer's field glimpsed from a car window might have borne witness to the last gasps of a bloody battle, an event so terrible the people swore it could never be forgotten. An eroded mound under a stand of trees might once have been the holy of holies, a sacred place worth travelling weeks to reach, for generations of ancient people.

In the landscape and in overlooked museum cabinets, archaeological treasures of profound complexity wait to be noticed. When you stop and look, magic happens. These wonders transport you into the secret lives of ancient people. These wonders are the stuff of this book.

In Britain's past we have cannibals, shamans, sun-, moon- and water-worshippers. We have Christian initiations and pagan bog sacrifices. We have mummies, mandrakes and magic. Britain boasts a depth of puzzling archaeology unrivalled anywhere else in the world. At least, that's what I think. Maybe it's because we have such a variety of landscapes, or unfathomable weather. Maybe it's because over the millennia so many different peoples have shaped this island, and made their marks in the landscape and on artefacts. Whatever it is, the mysterious past is what got me into archaeology in the first place. The day I went for an interview at Cambridge University as a nervously eager teenager, news of the discovery of Seahenge (page 60) had just been announced. I sat in a wing-backed armchair with an eminent scholar (Professor Chris Scarre, now at Durham University) and for half an hour we discussed how we might solve the riddle 'What the heck is it and what the heck is it for?' I was hooked. The fact that we're still not sure about the answers to those questions is neither here nor there.

Above The Desborough Mirror is one of the finest pieces of Iron Age Celtic art ever found. One side of the bronze was highly polished to produce a reflective surface. The back, pictured, is a riot of scrolls and coils forming a lyre shape. Decorated mirrors like this are uniquely British.

Even the best-known sites, studied for hundreds of years, continue to confound our search for explanation. Every generation of researchers unearths a little more of the picture or offers a new theory that creeps us closer to the truth . . . and then bam, a piece of evidence, a new radiocarbon date, a compelling anthropological comparison and we're back to the drawing board. Just like the people who built these sites and used these artefacts, they're complex, contrary and defy easy explanation. But that's exactly the reason they draw us in in the first place. It's why people love history and archaeology.

There's nothing like touching an artefact last used by someone alive 4,000 years ago, or standing in the doorway of an ancient house where the residents buried a mummified corpse under their floor. Hiking across a windswept moor to explore a stone row that leads to something or somewhere that – at least to my modern eyes – is invisible, is exciting. Standing at the top of a rocky outcrop, with my foot in a footstep shape that made men into kings, entwines my life with those of my forebears.

Archaeology is often focused on the how – and modern scientific techniques have answered many pressing questions. But I invite you to explore the more elusive question: Why? Why did Viking settlers in Cumbria carve Christian crosses with pagan gods (page 207)? Who built Aberdeenshire's stone altars (page 35) and carved Yorkshire's shamanic headdresses (page 57)? Why did ancient people in the west Highlands whittle a girl goddess by a lake (page 31) and people in Kent

bury a fancy golden cup in a mound (page 108)? Why did someone pee into a bottle in seventeenth-century London, then bury it in the cellar (page 92)? Our forebears had different gods and different priorities. They saw the world in a different way. And yet despite the distance, there are threads of meaning that link us, between generations and beyond cultures. It's like looking into a fairground hall of mirrors. It's disorienting, and yet we recognise something in the reflection. The right to stand puzzled, awe-struck, moved or uplifted in the presence of this strange and secret history, belongs to all of us.

In this book we head off on a loose geographical journey around the British Isles, starting in the far north east, on the Orkney Islands, and finishing in the far north west, in the Outer Hebrides. We leap between time periods – the oldest thing in this book is 33,000 years old (Paviland Cave Burial, page 177), the youngest is from 1916 (Headington Mandrake, page 136). If you want to visit these places and artefacts in the flesh – which I urge you to do – look online for access and opening times. If you can't head out, then digital resources can give you cutting-edge 3D models, aerial films and up-close-and-personal views of some of the most staggering things from Britain's past. There are suggested websites at the back of the book.

This book is full of Britain's secrets. These places and the stories they tell are very ancient, yet strangely timeless. Enjoy.

Mary-Ann

Below The Stones of Stenness in Orkney were once encircled by an oval bank and ditch, and a large fireplace was built in the centre of the enclosure. It's part of a complex ceremonial landscape that puzzles and compels in equal measure.

Timeline

DATE	PERIOD	EVENTS
2.6 million years ago – 9000 BC	**Paleolithic** *Early Stone Age*	**200,000 years ago** *Homo sapiens* evolve in Africa **31,000 BC** Earliest known human burial in Britain – *page 177* **26,000 BC** Last Neanderthals die out in Spain **15,000 BC** Gough's Cave bones – *page 157* **10,000 BC** First evidence of farming in the world
9000 BC – 4000 BC	**Mesolithic** *Middle Stone Age*	**9300–8500 BC** Hunters living at Star Carr – *page 57* **6200 BC** Posts aligning to Midsummer sunrise erected at Bryn Celli Ddu – *page 195* **6000 BC** Doggerland floods, making Britain an island
4000 BC – 2400 BC	**Neolithic** *Late Stone Age*	**4000 BC** First evidence of farming in Britain **3500 BC** Trethevy Quoit – *page 167* **3300 BC** Westray Wifey – *page 16* **3000 BC** First phase of building Stonehenge – *page 115* **3000 BC** Possible birth of the Fortingall Yew – *page 42* **2500 BC** Stonehenge sarsen stones erected
2400 BC – 800 BC	**Bronze Age**	**2400 BC** New 'Beaker' people arrive from continental Europe; earliest evidence of Bronze metal working in Britain **2400 BC** Silbury Hill begun – *page 125* **1700 BC** Ringlemere Gold Cup – *page 108* **1200 BC** Domestic horses introduced to Britain **1200 BC** Uffington Horse – *page 133* **c.900 BC** Must Farm village destroyed by fire – *page 71*
800 BC – AD 100	**Iron Age**	**800 BC** Earliest evidence of iron-working metallurgy **400 BC** 'Celtic' art traditions develop across Europe **c.100 BC** Penbryn Spoons – *page 188* **100 BC** Maiden Castle earthworks extended – *page 148* **70 BC** Snettisham Great Torc – *page 67* **55/54 BC** Attempted invasion of Britain by Julius Caesar
AD 43 – 410	**Roman**	**AD 43** Roman invasion of Britain **AD 40–60** Colchester Face Pot – *page 75* **AD 60/61** Queen Boudicca's revolt against the Romans **AD 122** Construction begins on Hadrian's Wall – *page 45*

DATE	PERIOD	EVENTS
AD 43 – 410	Roman	**AD 313** Roman Emperor Constantine converts to Christianity **AD 43–410** Cirencester Mother Goddesses – *page 139* **late 300s** First Angle and Saxon invasions and raids **AD 410** Fall of the Western Roman Empire
AD 400 – 1100	**Early Medieval** *Includes Anglo-Saxon 410–800* *Viking 800–1100*	**AD 432** St Patrick arrives in Ireland **AD 449** Angles and Saxons arrive in England **AD 450–650** Cornish elites at Tintagel trade with Greece, Syria and Turkey – *page 173* **AD 500–700** Aberlemno Pictish Stones – *page 39* **AD 600–700** Staffordshire Hoard deposited – *page 204* **AD 600–700** Baldehildis Seal – *page 74* **AD 793** First Viking attack on Lindisfarne Monastery, Northumbria **AD 842** Picts and the Gaels united under Kenneth MacAlpin, the birth of Alba – *page 225* **AD 928** Vale of York Cup – *page 211* **1053** Timbers of Greensted Church raised – *page 91*
1066 – 1500	**Medieval**	**1066** Norman invasion **1086** Domesday Book completed **1096–9** First Christian crusade to the Holy Land **1140** Kilpeck Sheela Na Gig – *page 181* **1170** Thomas à Becket murdered at Canterbury Cathedral **1275** St Michael's Tower, Glastonbury Tor – *page 151* **1348** Black Death in England kills 1.5 million people **1300s** Troston Demon – *page 83* **1300s** Wenhaston Doom Painting – *page 80*
1500 – 1800	**Post Medieval**	**1536–40** Henry VIII establishes Church of England and dissolves the monasteries **1590/1** First Shakespeare play performed in London **1600** Guildhall Witch Bottle – *page 92* **1666** Great Fire of London **1697** St Peter's, Dunwich, one of the town's last churches, falls into the sea – *page 79* **1742** Royston Cave rediscovered – *page 97*
1800 – present day	**Modern**	**1892** Wenhaston Doom painting rediscovered – *page 80* **1914-18** First World War **1916** Headington Mandrake – *page 136* **1939–45** Second World War **1988** Thames River witch bottle discovered – *page 92*

Map

Westray Wifey

A tiny goddess from the wild Northern Isles

Westray, Orkney

Right A figure found in the midden, or rubbish heap, surrounding a 5,000-year-old house in Orkney. Do the circles at the shoulders represent breasts or buttons?

This is the earliest representation of the human form ever found in Scotland. It's at least 5,000 years old, made from a tiny piece of sandstone, just 41 mm (1⅝ in) tall and 31 mm (1¼ in) wide.

At its shoulders are two circles, possibly breasts (hence her being a 'wife', or 'wifey', rather than a man), and on the back is a finely scored lattice that suggests clothing. But it's the face that gets you. The wifey peers out from pinprick eyes, with a faint 'M' denoting a brow, and a four-lined hash symbol for nose and mouth. None of the lines are deep, and even if it was once covered in some kind of pigment, the decoration wouldn't have stood out.

The figure was found in the midden (rubbish) layers at a farmstead on the Links of Noltland, on Westray island in Orkney, and dates to the Neolithic era (late Stone Age), around 3300–2500 BC. Just like the more famous Skara Brae, this village had a number of linked buildings made of stone with central hearths and stone dressers. The residents used their rubbish to insulate the sides of their homes, eventually making the village semi-subterranean. Amid the rotted waste, the archaeologists found this figurine. They've since found more wifeys: the second is made of clay and is missing its head; the third is lumpier, but retains a clear head/torso arrangement and the same little eyes.

Was this place particularly attached to wifeys, or is just an accident that three were found here, and none anywhere else? And how did they end up in the rubbish heap? They could have been lost or dropped, or – perhaps more likely – placed in the midden intentionally, possibly as offerings or talismans for luck, fertility or to ward off evil. Maybe there were originally wifeys everywhere, but just the ones that ended up in the midden survived.

There's no wear pattern that would suggest the figures were strung as pendants, and the bases are a bit wonky, so they're not obviously designed to stand up as statues. The features engraved into the stones are fine, and they don't look as though they were heavily handled. Maybe they were made solely to be deposited.

So-called 'Venus figurines' have been discovered across Asia and Europe, from the Neolithic and even earlier. The oldest discovered so far, the Venus of Hohle Fels, from Germany, is a staggering 35,000 years old. These figures are grouped together because they've got obvious female sexual characteristics – breasts, hips, bottoms and vulvas. But the truth is we don't know what they were used for, and we don't know if this Wifey should be classed as a 'Venus'.

The final mystery is whether this figure is really a 'wifey' at all. The two little marks at the shoulders may be buttons for clothes, rather than breasts or nipples. So perhaps the figure is wearing a cloak – which could be worn by a man. And of course if this is a representation of some form of spirit, god or ancestor, who's to say they conform to a binary gender of man or woman at all?

Ness of Brodgar

A monumental heart of ancient power

Mainland, Orkney

Left Five-thousand-year-old stone walls running in every direction.

Orkney is a small place, and these islands never had a huge population. But despite their small numbers and the remote location, the people who lived here 5,000 years ago packed quite a cultural punch.

Because ancient features were built in stone they've survived relatively well. It means you can go and visit the 5,000-year-old villages of Skara Brae and Barnhouse, where stone dressers and fireplaces are still *in situ*; you can walk into the oldest standing house in northern Europe on the tiny island of Papa Westray (constructed about 3600 BC), and journey to the formidable and numerous communal tombs including Maeshowe on Mainland, Midhowe on Rousay and Isbister on South Ronaldsay (page 25). It's clear that strange and powerful things happened here, and the people invested a lot of their time in the sacred and spiritual side of life.

On Orkney Mainland, between the iconic stone monuments of the Ring of Brodgar and the Stones of Stenness, and flanked by the Loch of Harray (freshwater) on one side, and the Loch of Stenness (seawater) on the other, there's a narrow strip of land just a couple of hundred metres wide and only 5 m (16 ft) above sea level. Many archaeologists had noticed the unusual rise of the land in a field next to a bungalow at the tip of the Ness of Brodgar, but it was only in 2003 that they had a chance to explore. They discovered the standing walls of ancient buildings running in every direction, dating from around 3500–2450 BC. This was during the Neolithic era (late Stone Age), when people were farming the land, growing wheat and barley and raising pigs, sheep and cattle. But this wasn't a normal farming village, and these weren't ordinary houses. The buildings were massive, with surviving painted and decorated stonework. They boasted stone tile roofs – the earliest ever discovered in Britain – and multiple hearths. Generation after generation built on the foundations of the buildings that had

Above Decorated stonework: fashionable home furnishing or sacred, mystic art?

come before, and the whole site was hemmed in by huge walls, up to 6 m (20 ft) thick, that formed complete barriers across the land at both the northern and southern ends. And then, around 2450 BC, for some reason, the site was abandoned.

In Neolithic times, when the Ness was an active site of ritual, the sea levels were lower. The Loch of Stenness was probably actually a salt marsh rather than the clear body of water that it is now, with boggy ground dotted with deeper pools. The Loch of Harray would have been smaller too. Tantalisingly, sonar surveys show that there are archaeological features on the drowned land either side. Archaeologists have now excavated this site for more than seventeen years, but reckon they've only revealed a tenth of it so far.

Structure 1 was constructed around 3000 BC. It's square-ish with rounded corners, made from neat drystone walls of the local sandstone. It was built and rebuilt a number of times.

Structure 8 was also large. It's a long, rounded rectangle oriented north–south and, bizarrely, it has six hearths; it's not clear whether these were all in use at the same time, and if so, for what purpose. It has given up some extraordinary artefacts, including polished stone and whalebone maceheads (a form of hammer) and pieces of decorated stone, incised with diamonds, zigzags and deeply carved cup marks. Intriguingly, when some of the buildings at the Ness were rebuilt, the builders intentionally laid some of the carved stones with their decoration facing inwards. Perhaps these pieces were created in order to be discarded or sacrificed (a bit like the Westray Wifey, page 16). Some of Structure 8's walls were also painted. We know this because, amazingly, the paint has survived. There are traces of black, white and red, and analysis shows that the red paint was made from haematite, a type of red ochre, probably ground up and mixed with milk or egg to make it stick.

Perhaps the most baffling building is Structure 10. It was built on top of part of Structure 8, in around 2900 BC. It was huge, 25 m (82 ft) long and 19 m (62 ft) across. Standing stones were erected to flank the east-facing entrance way and the whole thing was covered with a vast flagstone roof. The walls still stand to a height of 1 m (3 ft) and they're a staggering 4 m (13 ft) thick. An enclosure wall encircled this vast building, creating another layer between the outside world and whatever sanctum existed within. Inside was a central fireplace and at the threshold of the building, a vast stone laid flat in the earth.

The building (surely a temple?) was remodelled, probably to shore up some unstable walls, less than a hundred years after it was first built. These walls hold strange secrets of their own. A woman's arm bone was buried within them during the rebuilding phase. Another bone, possibly from the same woman, was under a different wall, along with cows' legs, a decorated stone slab and a carved stone ball (like the Towie

Ball, page 32). Are the arm bones positioned so they could hold up the walls of the temple? Not only is the potential symbolic value of these bones intriguing, they're even more significant because the Ness is an unusually 'clean' site when it comes to human remains. In the twenty-first century, we tend not to live among scattered human remains, with bones in ditches, rubbish heaps or in the dusty corners of our homes. But Neolithic sites are different – they've often got human bones dotted about, some intentionally placed or buried, others seemingly just knocking around. It may be because the bones haven't survived very well, or because the Ness of Brodgar is different, but it's clear the abundance of human remains we've come to expect in sites of this period is missing.

Despite the magnificent strangeness, the Ness was lived in. So far, more than 80,000 fragments of pottery storage jars, drinking cups and

Below The complexity of the site, and the thickness of the walls, laid bare. On the left is the saltwater Loch of Stenness; on the right, the freshwater Loch of Harray. They conceal even more archaeology.

Above The Ring of Brodgar was constructed around 2500 BC. Were the people erecting these stones the same people who had a massive barbeque and then destroyed the Ness?

bowls have been retrieved, including plenty of pieces that are still coloured with their original red ochre wash. You can't radiocarbon date the pottery itself, but you can date the fat that's been absorbed into the pottery from the food it held, and radiocarbon date burnt food residue inside the pots. Thankfully, the residents of the Ness did their share of burning the dinner, and it means that we've got dates – the earliest pottery was made around 3600–3300 BC – and Grooved Ware pottery, a form with bands of elaborate decoration around the vessel, starts to be made around 3100 BC. Grooved ware pottery is found across Britain and Ireland, and these early dates suggest the style actually originated here in Orkney. The assumption has often been that new pottery styles developed on continental Europe, eventually reached southern Britain and then spread to fringes like Orkney. But this evidence proves such preconceptions to be false. 'Civilisation' did not begin elsewhere before spreading here. The Ness shows us that Orkney was a centre of innovation and its people enjoyed powerful networks of exchange and influence. And it shows that others wanted to adopt it; pieces of grooved ware are found in the earliest phases of building at Stonehenge, for example.

On the southern side of the site, the boundary known as the Lesser Wall still stands to almost 2 m (6 ft) in height. Five thousand years ago the Stones of Stenness (see the picture on pages 8–9) would have faced this formidable wall across a narrow channel of water. Just 150 m (500 ft) beyond Stenness is Barnhouse village, comprising at least fifteen Neolithic houses that were built and used between 3100–2750 BC. Barnhouse also has its own mysterious temple structure – a rounded square with unusually thick walls – similar to Ness Structure 10: there's an outer encircling path, a square inner chamber with what appears to be a hearth at the centre and, utterly bizarrely, another hearth square in the middle of the doorway. To enter you'd have to walk through the fireplace.

Were the people on the Stenness/Barnhouse side of the water the same as the ones on the Ness? Or was the water channel the demarcating line between rival tribes or clans? Are all these monuments the result of megalithic one-upmanship? Perhaps the North Folk of the Ness built this monumental, holy village at the watery edge of their territory, with that hugely thick wall both to conceal and simultaneously boast of their activities. Just on the other side of the water, at the edge of their own territory, the tribe of Barnhouse looked on. They built the Stones of Stenness to stand tall against the Ness folk, and when the village of Barnhouse was abandoned around 2900–2750 BC, the people decided to build their own showstopper elsewhere, constructing Maeshowe tomb 1000 m (3,300 ft) to the south-east.

Much of this is speculation of course, and the calibration curve that translates radiocarbon decay times into actual dates is rather flat at this point in prehistory. It means that the dating can't be rendered more accurately until alternative methods are refined. And even then, we won't be able to recover the emotion, ambition and stories that must have been needed to get people to make and remake these mysterious sites time and again for some fifty generations or more.

At some moment between 2465–2360 BC, the remains of around 400 cows' legs were laid in the narrow passageway around Structure 10 on the Ness. Most of the bones had been split lengthways, suggesting people were eating the marrow as well as the meat, and all the bones were deposited at the same time – which represents a staggering number of cattle to slaughter, butcher and eat in one go. Inside the building, which had already been intentionally filled with rubble and rubbish, the people laid an upturned cow's head, and a short time later, whole bodies of red deer were put into the passage on top of the cows. And then Structure 10 was torn down. The mass slaughter of hundreds of full-grown cattle represents a huge expenditure of resources and a once-in-a-lifetime act of conspicuous consumption. Was this the wealth of one hugely influential elite family from the 'North Folk', or a tribute from people far and wide – including from beyond the water to the south? Was the feast in celebration, perhaps to mark a marriage or the end of a dispute? Or was it a collective act of prayer or despair, perhaps upon the death of a chief or a disaster?

This final dramatic destruction-feast at Structure 10 appears to be the last thing that happened within the monumental walls of the Ness site. But just a few hundred metres north, the Ring of Brodgar, a large stone circle and henge, was constructed around 2500 BC. Can it be coincidence that the dates for the start of the Ring and the end of the Ness are close? The Ring originally had sixty stones forming a circle 104 m (340 ft) across, set within a circular bank and ditch that was originally more than 7 m (23 ft) deep and dug into solid bedrock. The tallest stones are almost 5 m (16 ft) tall, and geological analysis shows that they've been quarried and brought from different outcrops across Orkney. Maybe the people dragging stones to Brodgar were also the people eating beef barbecue at the Ness? Were they people from families who'd lived here for generations, or were they new folk staking a claim to this ancient and powerful landscape? At this point, we just don't know.

The biography of this place is staggeringly complex, and its relationship with the surrounding sites even more so. What's certain is that every season of excavation on the Ness is likely to prompt another rewrite of the story of the Neolithic – in Orkney, across Britain and Ireland, and beyond.

Tomb of the Eagles

Where the ancestors lie with eagles

South Ronaldsay, Orkney

Left The interior of the 5,000-year-old tomb, with vertical stone stalls that create separate compartments. This was a place for people, eagles and ancestors.

Isbister is on a wind-blasted clifftop on South Ronaldsay island in Orkney. It's stark and awe-inspiring on a sunny summer's day; in the grip of winter, you feel as though you're clinging on to the edge of the world.

A stone's throw from the cliff edge, a low earthen mound conceals a tomb that holds the secrets of the ancient dead. The site was discovered in 1958, when a drystone wall was unearthed in a place where no one had any memory of ever building anything. The farmer investigated and found a cache of buried treasures – polished stone axeheads, a macehead, a knife blade made from chert stone and a little black jet button. And next to that, there was a stone chamber, stuffed with human skulls.

In style, this 5,000-year-old Neolithic tomb is a hybrid – the main rectangular chamber is divided by vertical flagstones to create stalled compartments, like an old-fashioned stable. But it also has three small side-cells coming off the main chamber, like the ones at the Maeshowe tomb, just up the road on Orkney Mainland. Normally, tombs are either one type or the other – at Isbister, it's both at once.

Isbister is unique in many other ways too, and the evidence is hard to interpret. Look online, and you'll read that there are the remains of at least 342 people jumbled together. But recent reassessment of the thousands of bones retrieved during excavations suggests that we can only be absolutely certain that it housed the remains of 85 people. Even though this figure is far lower, it's still the largest human bone assemblage and the greatest number of individuals recovered from any Neolithic tomb in the country. From the radiocarbon dating, we think the tomb was actively used for a thousand years, from around 3300 BC until some time around 2400–2200 BC, when the chamber was intentionally filled with rubble and its entrance passage sealed up.

Even though men, women and children's bodies are found in the tomb, there's a greater number of men than women, and more young

Above A quarter of the skulls show evidence of serious violence, and many others have congenital abnormalities. The forehead bones of this skull are unusually thickened.

adults than older people or children. And significantly, some of the men, women and children had been hit in the head, very hard. A quarter of the skulls had damage caused by heavy blows from stones or maceheads, as well as wounds from sharp-bladed weapons like spears or axes. The wounds don't appear to be the result of a ritual or sacrifice, because they're too variable. Some have been split in two, others have splinters of bone bent inwards but with evidence of healing, indicating the person survived the trauma. One woman's skull had three different blunt force wounds, as well as a dislocated jaw, but she'd survived each enough to heal. How should we make sense of this? Were they being attacked in inter-tribal warfare? Fighting each other? Was this wild island a hotbed of murder and domestic abuse? It certainly demands that we recalibrate the picture we might hold of peaceful farmers living together quietly. But because we don't have the skeletons of the rest of the community, we can't tell whether these tomb bones are typical of the whole society – where one in four people was the victim of a potentially fatal assault – or whether this was a special group, with a special experience of interpersonal violence.

Perhaps even more strange is that the tomb didn't just contain human remains. It also contained eagles. The talons and bones of at least fourteen white-tailed sea eagles, native to the neighbouring sea cliffs, were found in the tomb along with the jumbled human bones.

The chambered tomb of Cuween Hill has an intriguing parallel. It's 42 km (26 miles) north, near Finstown Village on Orkney Mainland, and boasts human remains alongside the skulls of twenty-four small, straight-snouted dogs. Isbister tomb is known as the 'Tomb of the Eagles'. So, inevitably, Cuween is now known as the 'Tomb of the Beagles'.

There's a theory that these tombs belonged to different tribes, each with a totem animal – a species that was spiritually important, even sacred. Perhaps the animals were thought to protect or guide the person or community they were linked to, acting as spiritual messengers between the people and gods, and as potent sacrifices in times of need. Maybe the head injuries were caused by fights between Eagle people and Beagle people.

But further analysis of the radiocarbon dating throws us a curve ball. At both Isbister and Cuween the animal remains appear to date from significantly later than the original construction and earliest burials – at least 500 years later, in fact. So these were definitely not totemic deposits made by the people who first built tombs. It may be that later people reusing and reinterpreting the sites did have a special relationship with specific animals in the landscape. Was this a new religion, or a new expression of a continued belief? We don't know.

Maybe the best way to think of a tomb like this is not as a burial monument, but like a parish church – a venue for social rituals around birth, marriage, death, harvest, Midwinter and many others, as well as a place for personal prayers.

The closing of the tomb around 2400 BC came at the same time that metal-working technology was first introduced to the British Isles by people from the Continent. The people who had command of this technology may well have also had the power to transform society in other ways. Maybe the introduction of eagle remains to the tomb, and then the complete decommissioning of the site, were responses to these new people and their new ways.

To enter Isbister tomb now, you lie on your back on a small wooden trolley, and pull yourself head first 3 m (10 ft) along the low passage into the grave's heart. As you begin to move, take a moment to remember how much we simply don't know; the Tomb of the Eagles refuses to be boiled down to a single, coherent narrative. People defy simplicity.

Below The entrance stonework has been restored, but the long, low entrance passage is original. You need to crawl or use a trolley to get inside.

Sculptor's Cave

Sea-cliff cavern festooned with the dead

Moray

Left The cave entrance, where the majority of juvenile skulls and jaws were discovered. Gold hair ornaments on the floor suggest the children's heads were whole when they were first placed here.

The cave is at the base of cliffs on the south shore of the Moray Firth. Only accessible at low tide, two long passageways lead you to a large echoing cavern, deep within the rock.

There are Pictish stone carvings and some modern graffiti. Ignore that, and focus instead on the archaeological layers from the late Bronze Age, around 1000 BC. It's here we find dead children's heads, suspended by the cave entrance, and scattering the floor.

Excavating in the 1920s, archaeologists found thousands of human bones on the cave floor, along with evidence of stone hearths, burned soil and metalwork, including gold hair ornaments. They noted the surprising number of juvenile bones, particularly legs, skulls and pieces of jaw. The skull fragments and jaws were overwhelmingly in the cave's entrance passages. Some pieces of bone appeared polished, and one piece of skull had the feathery cut marks that you might make if you were trying to fillet a piece of meat. And that's the archaeologists' interpretation: at least part of the skull was intentionally de-fleshed.

We don't know if the children were intentionally killed, or whether they died of something else, and were then carried to the cave for the rituals. Once they were *in situ*, their bodies were curated – perhaps laid out on display or their flesh cut away and distributed. The heads appear to be the most important parts, and were carefully arranged at the entrance. Whether this display was for living human visitors, or for gods or spirits who were present in the cave, we don't know.

Modern ghost and horror stories attest to children's potent spiritual power – they can be innocent and pure, but they can also be demonic, dangerous and closer to the spirit world. Were these ancient kiddies in the cave dangerous? Did they have a job to do, guarding the living community, or intercessing on behalf of their families? Or were they innocents, blood sacrifices offered to appease the spirits, or ensure a good harvest?

For a long time it was thought that all the human bone from Sculptor's Cave was from the same period. But new work on the remains has revealed a bizarre new chapter for this cavern of the dead. There were in fact two distinct periods of activity, separated by a thousand years. The children's remains do come from the late Bronze Age, around 1000 BC, but a second set of remains, including six adults who were killed by having their heads chopped off, date to the Roman Iron Age, around 200 AD. These later remains have been interpreted as ritual executions, human sacrifices perhaps, in a place that was already steeped in ancient mystery. Later people wouldn't have known how their ancestors used the caves a thousand years before, but they would have seen the bones. And told stories.

Recent investigation has shown that other caves on this coast were also used for prehistoric death rituals. It's an enigmatic place, quietly beautiful now, but witness to thousands of years of strange ceremonies and powerful magic. Here, the past feels like a very strange country indeed.

Deskford Carnyx

An Iron Age horn for war

Moray

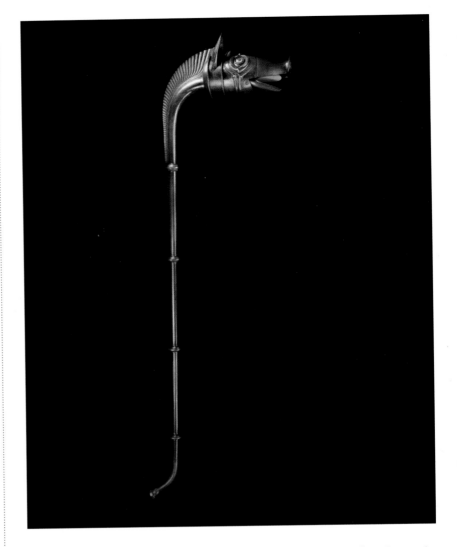

Above This is a replica of a long-necked, animal-headed Iron Age bronze horn known as a carnyx. The original was deposited in a bog, between AD 80 and 250, probably as a sacrificial offering to the gods. Only the boar-shaped bell survives, but from other fragmentary survivors, and more than a hundred depictions on coins, sculptures and ceramics, experts have been able to recreate this strange musical beast. Diodorus Siculus, the first-century BC Roman historian, described carnyces as 'war trumpets of a peculiar barbaric kind; they ... produce a harsh sound, which suits the tumult of wars'. Players held the horn vertically, so the boar would stand high above their heads. The harsh blasts were intended to rouse fear – or perhaps bravery – in those who heard its cry.

Ballachulish Figure

A contorted lakeside goddess

West Highlands

Above This spectral form, made from alder wood with quartz pebbles for eyes, was found in 1880 by the shores of Loch Leven. As the wood dried out, it cracked and distorted into this elongated oddity, but when new, around 600 BC, the face was rounded and the features were clearer – a life-size naked figure of a girl or goddess (possessing female genitalia, but undeveloped breasts), holding something in her hands (we can't be sure what). Within the wooden base was a small niche – perhaps for offerings. The goddess probably originally stood upright on a beach. Were statues like this a rarity in the Iron Age, or should we imagine a prehistoric world peppered with shrines and idols?

Towie
Stone Ball

*A game or a
sacred object?*

Aberdeenshire

These carved stone balls are immediately recognisable, and yet tantalisingly enigmatic. Archaeologists have now found around 500 of them across north-eastern Scotland, mostly in Aberdeenshire. This one is from Glaschul Hill, in Towie, Aberdeenshire. It weighs 500 g (18 oz), is just larger than a modern tennis ball and has four 'knobs'. Three of them are carved in intricate, eternal spirals and swirls. The fourth is completely blank. We have no idea what they're for.

The Towie Ball was discovered by workmen cutting a new drain into the side of the hill around 1860. Archaeologists have since found other carved balls in more secure contexts; on the floors of the Neolithic houses at Skara Brae in Orkney and under a huge stone buttress at the Ness of Brodgar (page 19). Given this evidence, we can be pretty sure they were made by people in the late Stone Age, perhaps around 3000 BC.

These stone balls share a number of characteristics. Most of them boast six circular knobs, carved to stand proud from the form of the sphere. Some balls have as few as three, and others are pimpled with hundreds. A little less than a sixth of the balls have designs carved into their surfaces – all the other balls are entirely blank. The patterns on the decorated stones are remarkably similar to the art motifs – spirals, chevrons, concentric circles – found on rare carved stones at Welsh passage graves Barclodiad Y Gawres and Bryn Celli Ddu (page 195). They, in turn, seem to echo the art styles more commonly found on tombs in Ireland.

So why did people living in Aberdeen 5,000 years ago decide to carve small rocks with the same decoration that other people carved into megalithic temples and tombs? It might be something to do with portability – perhaps the people of Aberdeenshire were more mobile than their Irish counterparts and so they'd carry their holiest rocks with them. Or maybe the regular folk were just as settled as the rest of Neolithic Britain, but the people entitled to use these rocks were the ones on the move – wandering priests, perhaps.

All the stones have been created from a pebble or rough rock by 'pecking' at the stone with another rock, slowly knocking off the edges to form a ball, then marking out all the complex geometric patterns then grinding again to shape and refine the lines. The techniques would have been familiar and aren't technically challenging. But they are time-consuming, and have been executed to an extraordinary degree of precision. It probably means that these balls aren't part of a pastime or game, unless the game itself indicated some level of status and exclusivity.

Other suggestions include use as a ceremonial slingshot or as a weapon for delivering a fatal blow to the skull of a sacrificial victim. Or maybe they were used in some method of divination, like the strange spoons of Penbryn (page 188)? Or maybe they were thought to contain spirits or memories. If a wandering priest could carry the stone balls, and therefore hold the history and tell the stories, they would command great power.

Tomnaverie Recumbent Stone Circle

A window to the heavens

Aberdeenshire

Left The massive recumbent and two flankers at Tomnaverie. The ground under the recumbent has been carefully shaped, but not to make it flat. Is this an altar, or a celestial viewing window?

It sits up on a wide hilltop, just east of the Cairngorm mountains. The views are endless, and the skies massive. This may just be the reason someone built this monument, a recumbent stone circle, 4,500 years ago.

There are just 100 circles of this type, and they're only found in the north-east of Scotland, mostly in Aberdeenshire. Their most striking feature is a massive stone lying down on its side, the 'recumbent', in the southern or south-western part of the circle. The ground surface beneath the recumbent is always carefully smoothed, but strangely, not always to make the top side flat, Sometimes the surface echoes the line of the landscape horizon behind it.

On either side of the recumbent are two tall standing stones – these are the 'flankers'. Often one is tall and narrow, and the other shorter and fatter. The rest of the stones circle out in descending height order, so the smallest stone is at the far side, standing opposite the massive recumbent.

We know that the Tomnaverie hilltop was used for funeral pyres around 2500 BC, on the cusp of the transition between Stone Age and Bronze Age. You can still see the remains of the stone cairn that was built over the bone fragments and charcoal from the pyre. Then, shortly afterwards, the builders came back and constructed this stone circle around the cairn. More than a thousand years later, new people came here and buried someone's cremated remains at the centre of the by-then ancient cairn and circle. Most unusually, cremated remains were also added to the monument in medieval times, between 1400–1600 AD – a staggering 4,000 years after its first use.

There are many theories about recumbent stone circles (RSCs). Some people think the massive recumbents represent blocked gateways, either to keep things in the circle, or hold them out. Others suggest the recumbent and flankers are an altar, or a viewing window, either of the

landscape beyond, or for observations of the moon, stars and planets, and
the performance of rituals related to these celestial events.

Certainly, the view of the mountain Lochnagar seen through the
flankers is striking. And if Tomnaverie is aligned with the heavens, it seems
to be focused on the winter night sky. Looking from the north-eastern side
of the circle across to the recumbent, the sun sets on to the 'altar' stone
every day between October and February. The winter full moon travels above
it, and on the night of the Midwinter solstice, the red stars Aldebaran and
Betelgeuse set to the right, the white star Sirius sets to the left, while Orion's
Belt sets on top of it.

This strange and ancient circle contains many stones with inclusions of
quartz. In moonlight and firelight they would have glimmered and twinkled
like the orbs in the sky above. Without doubt, this is a circle of the night,
and a circle of death. But it's also surely a circle of cyclical, seasonal life.

Aberlemno Pictish Stones

Ancient symbols that have never been deciphered

Angus

Left The Serpent Stone, with snake, Double-Disc and Z-Rod, and mirror and (less discernable) comb at the bottom. It might spell out a Pictish leader's name from 1,500 years ago, if only we knew how to read it. The back of this stone also has prehistoric ritual cup marks – perhaps a reason the Picts decided to use this stone for carving in the first place.

The red sandstone monolith leans gently, its ancient face covered in strange, deeply carved symbols. At the top there's a dark snaking form. Then, a zigzag with linked discs positioned in the angles. At the base, there's a circular form that can best be described as resembling a looking-glass mirror. This is the Aberlemno 'Serpent Stone', and the carvings date to the 500s or early 600s AD. Just a few metres further along the grassy verge is another carved stone, and then another. A final enigma stands in the churchyard nearby. The village of Aberlemno is, for unknown reasons, blessed with one of the best collections of ancient Pictish art in existence.

The Picts are the almost-legendary race of people who lived in what's now north and eastern Scotland until the 900s AD. The Romans coined the name, from the Latin *picti*, meaning 'painted people'. It wasn't intended to be complimentary, but rather to describe their savage, barbarian ways. These Picts, the Roman writers said, fought naked but for their paint, and were happy to wade neck-deep through swamps in order to wage guerrilla warfare. They were battle-hardened, proud people, who thrived in the harsh northern lands beyond the Roman frontier.

We're not sure whether these warriors really were painted, and if they were, whether the Romans were describing body paint or tattoos. And we don't know what they called themselves at this time. At some point, however, they decided to take ownership of this Roman slur and began to call themselves the Picts.

The symbols carved on Pictish stones recur time and again, often in complex groups. They fall into three categories – everyday objects, abstract motifs and animals. The symbols are often found in pairs – the abstract Crescent and V-Rod, or the Double-Disc and Z-Rod, the more identifiable hammer and anvil pair, or a comb and mirror. Wolves, eagles, snakes and fish are frequently represented; the bear and the bull are

Above The Roadside cross-slab is carved on all sides, with worshipping angels either side of the cross, Pictish symbols, a hunting scene and the biblical King David fighting a lion. Early Christianity was entirely compatible with traditional Pictish culture.

seen less, and only ever appear alone. The most common animal is the mysterious Pictish Beast. It has a flat back, four curved limbs, a curving crest on its crown and a possible beak (or bill, or maybe even trunk). Some people think it's a dolphin, others see a chimera – a fantastical hybrid beast with features of many animals drawn into one.

These carved symbols are thought to be a form of writing, perhaps a simple version of hieroglyphs. There are too few symbols to be a whole language, but maybe they represent people's names, lineages, or places? Until we find the Scottish equivalent of the Rosetta Stone, we remain in the tantalising, mysterious dark.

From the late-600s, Pictish symbols were incorporated into beautifully executed, sophisticated patterns on 'cross-slabs' – a reflection of the increasing influence of Christianity. In the Aberlemno churchyard there's a mammoth slab of sandstone that was carved into a masterpiece in the early 700s AD. On one side is a huge elaborate Celtic cross, covered in swirling knotwork; interlaced animals biting snakes and a pair of hippocamp seahorses, their style imitating that of ancient Roman or Greek art. On the other side of the slab is the abstract Z-rod symbol, an archway shape and a triple-circle, and below, a depiction of a battle.

The stone shows long-haired warriors (probably the Picts) fighting helmeted warriors. At the bottom right there's a helmeted warrior lying or falling, his shield abandoned by his side, and a bird about to peck his face. This, we can assume, is the defeated enemy, left on the battlefield to be scavenged by carrion crows. If this is a memorial for a real battle, our best guess is that it's the infamous Battle of Dun Nechtain in 685 AD, which was fought between the Picts and the powerful Anglian king of Northumbria, Ecgfrith. The Venerable Bede, who was a young scholar at the time of the battle, says Ecgfrith 'rashly led an army to waste the province of the Picts . . . the enemy pretended to flee and so he was led into the defiles of inaccessible mountains, and annihilated, with a great body of the men he brought with him.'

The Picts fought battles with the Gaels from the west of Scotland, Celtic Britons from southern Scotland and Cumbria, as well as the powerful Anglians from the south. In the 800s Viking raiders also joined the fray, pushing in from strongholds on the Scottish islands and the northern mainland. (That's why Sutherland, in the far north of Scotland, is called the 'Southern Land' – it was named by people from Norway.)

In 839 AD the Vikings destroyed a combined army of Gaels and Picts, killing both the Gaelic and Pictish kings, and in 842 AD Cináed son of Alpín (now better known as Kenneth MacAlpin) became King of the Picts. He probably had heritage from both Pictish and Gaelic royal families, but his rule marks the start of a Gaelic domination of what was once Pictish land. So thorough was the Gaelic takeover that Cináed's accession is the moment many historians identify as the birth of Alba, the kingdom that led to the nation of Scotland. In the *Who's Who* of Scottish history, Gaelic lineage became more politically advantageous than Pictish lineage, so eventually even those people who were Picts left their Pictish identity behind.

The mysterious Picts haven't quite disappeared. The people are part of the ethnic mix that makes up modern Scotland, and traces of their language remain in place names containing elements like 'Aber' (river mouth, as in Aberdeen), 'Pit' (piece of land, as in Pitlochry) and 'Carden' (wood, as in Kincardine). But Pictish culture and their spoken language are largely lost, and these monoliths are now as close as we can get. The Aberlemno stones are covered with wooden boxes from the last working day of September to the first working day of April to protect the carvings from the worst ravages of winter. But for the rest of the year, they stand proudly, arrestingly, shouting in voices we barely understand.

Below Is this the battle of Dun Nechtain fought in AD 685, where long-haired Picts (on the left) defeated the powerful Anglian army (on horseback with helmets)? The churchyard cross-slab is a masterpiece of carved art.

Fortingall Yew

The mystical history of the oldest tree in Europe

Perthshire

This tree is the oldest living thing in Europe. We're not sure exactly how old, but it's definitely been around for at least 3,000 years. It could, possibly, even be a staggering 5,000 years old. This means that some time in the period between people burying their dead in Isbister tomb (page 25), and when people were dropping the Dagenham Idol in the River Thames (page 102), and bronze swords into Flag Fen (page 95) there was a little sprig that would become the Fortingall Yew.

The common yew – *Taxus baccata* – is notoriously difficult to date. They don't grow tree rings, their growth rate declines with age and they can continue to grow in separate fragments, even after the main centre of the tree has disappeared. This is what's happened in the churchyard at Fortingall. But our best guess to age a yew is still to measure it. The original tree was measured in the 1760s and found to be 16 m (52 ft) in girth; now there are two living fragments from that centre remaining. The biggest yew ever recorded was the Brabourne Yew in Kent, at 18 m (58 ft 6 in), and a similar-sized one lived in the churchyard at Sutton, in Winchester. They've both since died.

The site of Fortingall isn't entirely understood but it is decidedly ancient. When the old church was demolished in 1900, locals found fragments of early Christian grave slabs embedded in the walls, dating to the 600s AD. It suggests the old church was built from the ruins of an even older church. There's also archaeological evidence of some kind of enclosure around the area, which might be a monastic 'vallum' around the earliest church (a ditch that acted as both a physical and spiritual boundary from the outside world), It could be an even older boundary that existed before stories of Jesus ever reached these hillsides. What else – or who else – did it encircle, along with our ancient yew?

It seems obvious that the Church would embrace the yew as an embodiment of resurrection and (seemingly) everlasting life: they're evergreen, and when you cut them, they bleed red sap. But how do we explain the fact that many yew trees predate their nearest church by centuries, if not millennia? It seems likely that the prehistoric people of Britain considered the yew to be sacred. So when the first sermons were preached, it made sense to do it at a place the community already believed was special. The preachers came to Fortingall because the yew was there already.

In 1803, William Wordsworth, describing a yew tree in Lorton, Cumbria, said it 'stands single, in the midst / Of its own darkness, as it stood of yore.' The Fortingall Yew's caretakers are becoming concerned for its welfare. It's become famous; people visit, tie things into its branches and tear off twigs. The extraordinary tree has survived because it stood so long in the midst of its own darkness. Now it has a name, a Wikipedia page and fans. The Fortingall Yew's fame may prove to be the thing that sends it into the dark forever.

Right The Fortingall Yew is probably the oldest living thing in Europe.

42

Hooded Spirits on Hadrian's Wall

Genii Cucullati, the mysterious figures in cloaks

Northumberland

When we think about the Roman army, we often focus on battle formations, well-drilled troops and formidable weaponry. What gets less attention are the beliefs and practices of soldiers who were deeply superstitious and religiously observant.

So let's look beyond mighty Hadrian's Wall and focus, instead, on a tiny sandstone carving. It was found in a shrine near to Housesteads Roman Fort, dating to the early 200s AD. These are the Genii Cucullati, or 'Hooded Spirits'. They are found in threes (like the Mother Goddesses, page 139) and are always shrouded. The type of hooded woollen cloak they're wearing is a *birrus Britannicus*. This 'British cloak' was a prized export, mentioned in the Edict of Diocletian in 301 AD, which lists the finest goods traded across the whole of his empire. It rather suggests that Britain has always had a reputation when it comes to bad weather, but that we've also always been quite good at making premium wet-weather gear.

No inscriptions have ever been found with images of the Genii Cucullati in Britain, so it's difficult to know what they represent. Are they friendly protectors, or dangerous folk needing to be appeased? Some images show Genii carrying rounded objects that may be eggs. If so, perhaps they're linked to fertility or birth and rebirth. Other Genii appear to be armed with knives, so maybe they're also warriors or defenders. It's even speculated that the British tradition of ghostly sightings of hooded monks may be a Christianised remnant of these ancient hooded spirit beliefs.

This carving was probably part of a shrine, situated in the *vicus*, the civilian settlement that formed next to the main military complex. It was where the shops and services for civilians living around military installations were based. Housesteads was home to 800 well-drilled infantry troops recruited from the conquered peoples of modern

Belgium. From the third century it was also home to Frisian mercenaries (from modern-day Netherlands) stationed at Hadrian's Wall. Were these freelancers the ones who wanted to make offerings to the mysterious hooded men? Did they commission the shrine and pray for success, protection or fortune?

Inside the military fort at Housesteads, archaeologists have also discovered evidence of cult worship of an equally mysterious deity. Mithras was originally worshipped in Persia, but was adopted by Roman soldiers across the Empire. Normally he's depicted killing a mystical bull in a cave, but at Housesteads he's depicted being born out of an egg, rising naked with half the eggshell on his head, surrounded by the egg-shaped cosmos of all things. This is an odd amalgam, incorporating elements of Ancient Greek Orphic religion, and the temple is dedicated not to regular Mithras, but to Mithras Saecularis – 'Mithras, Lord of this Age'.

Housesteads was at the very limit of the Roman world, a frontier against perceived savages. But it wasn't just a place of warfare, it was richly religious and profoundly mystical. These men, seventeen centuries ago, worshipped at the physical and spiritual edge of the world.

Thornborough Henges

Yorkshire's secret monumental landscape

North Yorkshire

Right The low plateau between the Rivers Ure and Swale, flanked by the hills of Yorkshire's Pennine hills and the North York Moors, is home to the greatest concentration of prehistoric henge monuments in the British Isles. These linked henges at Thornborough – ceremonial spaces encircled by earth banks and ditches – are the centrepiece of this vast ritual landscape, created in the late Stone Age and Bronze Age. The henges align roughly north-west to south-east, and are joined together by wide earthwork avenues. Each henge is 240 m (787 ft) in diameter, and spaced 550 m (1,800 ft) apart from its neighbour. The slight dogleg in the alignment mirrors the three stars of Orion's Belt constellation. Coincidence? You decide. The real mystery is how such a significant archaeological landscape is so little known to the public.

Rudston Monolith

Britain's tallest standing stone

East Riding of Yorkshire

Above This is the tallest standing stone in Britain: 7.6 m (25 ft) high, with perhaps the same astonishing amount of stone below ground as above. What makes it even more arrestingly odd is that it's next to the village church, just 4 m (13 ft) from its north-eastern corner. The stone was probably erected around 1600 BC, during the Bronze Age, so it predates the church by around 2,700 years. When Christianity swept Britain in Anglo-Saxon times, the ancient pagan stone was transformed into a symbol of the new religion. There's a hole at its top that was probably drilled so the stone could hold a wooden cross, and it's likely to be the origin of the village name too – in Old English *rood* means 'cross', *stane* means 'stone': hence, Rood-Stane, or Rudston.

Roos Carr Figurines

Mysterious dolls from the Iron Age

East Riding of Yorkshire

Above In 1836, labourers cleaning out a ditch came across a little huddle of wooden figurines. These dolls are between 35–41 cm (13 ¾ –16 in) tall, made from yew wood, with pebbles for eyes, and sockets for wooden arms and their sizeable penises. Additional pieces form shields, boat paddles and a long, low boat with a serpent's head that the figures could fit in. Radiocarbon dating indicates they're 2,600 years old, from the early Iron Age. These tiny warriors are probably not toys, but could be votive offerings – perhaps asking for protection or giving thanks. There's evidence for human sacrifice elsewhere in the British Iron Age, so it's possible that these are symbolic human sacrifices. It's also possible that they don't represent people at all, but are, in fact, the gods themselves.

Ilkley Moor

Enigmatic prehistoric rock art landscape

West Yorkshire

Left The Badger Stone has 100 cup marks and concentric rings jostling for space, interlinked by grooves and gutters. The name probably originates from the adjacent ancient track used by traders, including medieval corn millers known as 'badgers'.

It takes a while, sometimes, to 'get your eye in', and catch British rock art. It isn't impressive like the famous cave paintings of Lascaux in France, with horses and bison galloping across a stone canvas. British rock art is small, nude carving that defies easy explanation. Many of the marks can be mistaken for natural dips and hollows in an otherwise unshaped stone – and analysis has shown that the carvers sometimes used the natural patterns, augmenting what was already there. But if you only ever try spotting prehistoric rock art in the landscape once – little circular bowls carved into earthfast boulders, enigmatic grooves, concentric rings – do it on Ilkley Moor.

The term 'British rock art' refers to stone engravings that date from 4000–1500 BC, the Neolithic to the middle Bronze Age. There are around 7,000 known rock art panels across Britain, and more are being discovered every year. They're found on large, earthbound rocks, rock outcrops and standing stones. They're also incorporated into tombs. The easiest way to find these enigmatic stones is to use an app and a ten-digit grid reference to guide you to the exact spot – details can be found online.

The fact that rock art is found on Ilkley Moor in great volumes (more than 400 panels found so far) might not be because it was a special spot back then, but rather, because it hasn't been developed for building or for intensive agriculture since. There may well have been rock art on the spot that's now Liverpool Lime Street station, in the middle of a farmer's wheat field in Warwickshire or under Big Ben. But of course, those rocks are long gone now.

The most common rock art motif is a circular 'cup mark', that's been pecked out with a harder hammer stone, and then ground down to form a smooth cup shape. The cups are often surrounded by concentric rings, making a 'cup-and-ring'. Sometimes they have a 'gutter' radiating out

from the centre and other times a cup-and-ring is linked by a 'groove' to another cup-and-ring. Ilkley Moor has some unique motifs too, including 'ladders' – parallel grooves with perpendicular 'rungs' – that are found on the Panorama Stone and the Barmishaw Stone. There's also a swastika, on the . . . Swastika Stone. It's the only one known in Britain, save for an incomplete (three-legged) swastika on the Badger Stone. The most compelling are the panels that exhibit a collection of motifs. The lines swirl and pop, and you feel your eye dancing across them, trying to find the meaning. British rock art is special because it's always more than the sum of its parts. The Pepperpot Stone is a perfect example – it's just a bunch of cup marks, but taken together, they transform a rock into a baffling but compelling ancestral artefact.

Of course, the big question is what were these carvings for?

Ilkley Moor was probably at least partly wooded when the carvings were made. The land wasn't peat-bound yet, and would have been farmed and grazed. The markings seem too small to be used as territorial markers – you'd only see them if you knew to look. But maybe they denoted boundaries that were more subtle; perhaps areas of the landscape only accessible to initiated people or to elders.

There are no clear patterns to the arrangements of the motifs, but they could be representations of stories or places, perhaps created or used by people in trances. Research suggests patterns like these are a universal output when the human brain is high on magic mushrooms. Maybe the patterns were used in ceremonies for divining the future by reading the marks made by pouring liquids – milk, oil, blood – on to the rocks. Or perhaps the act of making the pattern was the important thing, and the resulting 'art' was of no consequence. Whatever the truth, your guess is as good as the experts. And Ilkley Moor is a magical place to ponder the truth.

Star Carr

Shamans and hunters from 11,000 years ago

North Yorkshire

Left Red deer frontlets, with drilled holes and antlers halved along their lengths. Were the holes drilled to create eyeholes in a mask, or for tying the antlers on to make a headdress?

About 11,000 years ago, at the end of the last Ice Age, part of the Vale of Pickering in North Yorkshire was underwater. Researchers call it Lake Flixton, and it was 4 km (2½ miles) long and 2 km (1¼ miles) wide. You can't see the lake any more, but in winter the water table is sometimes just centimetres from the surface, and if you jump, the ground wobbles like a jelly. The water-logging is what's made this place such an archaeological treasure trove, because it preserves organic matter that would otherwise rot into oblivion.

The jewel in this watery crown is Star Carr, a promontory on the lake's western edge. It was first excavated in the 1940s when the diggers found flint, bone, antler and wood that had been used and shaped by the first permanent inhabitants of Britain, in around 9300 BC. These were Mesolithic (middle Stone Age) hunter-gatherers who had walked over the low-lying Doggerland region (now under the North Sea), from what's now the Netherlands and Denmark. They came following grazing animals like deer, elk and wild cattle, and found land rich with woodland materials, fish and meat. At first, excavators thought Star Carr must have been a temporary hunting camp, used by unsophisticated people wandering across the landscape, moving as the animals and their whim took them. The overwhelming evidence now indicates that these were a knowledgeable people with seasonal and geographical expertise. They were able to thrive in this new post-glacial world. Star Carr was regularly occupied between 9300–8500 BC; it was home for generations.

We find traces of burning from around 9000 BC, suggesting the people were selectively burning vegetation to encourage new plant shoots to grow, which would draw grazing animals to prime hunting spots. Around 8950 BC, the people started to construct layered wooden platforms on the lakeshore to make a series of rough jetties. The longest extended more than 17 m (56 ft) into the reeds at the edge of the lake.

The discovery of a wooden paddle suggests that these people used boats, perhaps constructed like a coracle, with a waterproof animal hide hull over a bowl-shaped wicker frame. These jetties may be the start of the British love affair with boating. They also built thatched tepee or dome hut houses, evidenced by rings of post-holes and flattened central areas.

What really makes Star Carr stand out from all the other Mesolithic sites we know about, are the antler 'frontlets'. These are the skulls of red deer that have been purposefully shaped to create what we think are headdresses or masks. Thirty-three have been discovered in what would have been the shallow water of the lake, intentionally dropped into the water, perhaps after use. Nothing like these frontlets has ever been discovered anywhere else in Europe.

To construct a frontlet, the people broke off the rest of the skull keeping just the forehead, crown and antlers, and smoothed the bone edges. Then they drilled two holes into the skull and cut down the tines of the antlers. They didn't just cut the antlers off, they painstakingly carved away half of each antler longitudinally, splitting them along their length. They also carved off the thick burrs at the base of the antlers, where they join the skull. These are the hardest parts of the prongs, and the carving would have taken hundreds of hours of work for each frontlet. Why? Was it just to reduce the weight of the antlers, or was it some more mystical desire to make the antlers look strange and special?

We're not completely certain what the frontlets were used for, but it seems most likely that a thong or string was threaded through the two holes so they could be tied on to a person's head. They could have been used as hunting disguises, but most hunters don't think wearing horns on your head, tied under your chin, would help the stealthy movement required to creep up on wild animals and successfully dispatch them with a spear. What seems more likely from ethnographic comparison is that the hunter-gatherers of Star Carr practised some form of animistic religion, and these frontlets were used in ceremony and ritual that transformed the wearers into something more than human. Perhaps shamans wore them in rituals where they could leave their human bodies and transport into the world of the animals and spirits. In this alternate reality they could learn about the future, intercede on behalf of their community and seek wisdom from the animal-spirit world. Maybe they were used in initiation ceremonies, when young men and women transformed into a new 'type' of person, capable of leading a hunt, leaving home or getting married. The frontlets may well have been incorporated with other materials – skins, for example – to create a more complete costume.

The deer is a potent spiritual animal in many northern and European cultures. The Siberian mother goddess Rohanitsa has antlers and can give birth to both children and deer. The Sami reindeer people venerate the female reindeer goddess as a bringer of life at the time of the winter solstice. There are images dating from the late British Iron Age (around 100 BC) depicting Cernunnos, a god with antlers, and an antlered shaman can be seen on the Danish Gundestrup cauldron, which also dates to around 100 BC. In 1785, a western explorer drew a picture of a Mongolian shaman wearing an antler headdress almost identical to the ones found at Star Carr. In the picture he's dancing a ritual with a beater and drum. And even Father Christmas has magical deer that fly through time and space.

The water table of the Lake Flixton area is now changing and the 11,000-year-old bones, antlers and wood are beginning to rot away. Despite the extensive excavations at Star Carr, only 10 per cent of the lakeshore has been examined: that leaves 1.7 hectares (4¼ acres) of *terra incognita*. It's humbling to know that our shifting climate means that the ancient secrets of these shamans and hunters may be lost forever.

Below So far, ninety-three barbed harpoon points have been found. Made from deer antler, they were used to hunt animals and harpoon fish, and were then deposited in the water at the edges of the lake.

Seahenge

An upturned tree reaching beyond worlds

Norfolk

Right This extraordinary monument – an upside-down oak tree stump surrounded by a ring of fifty-five split oak posts – was 'planted' in 2049 BC during the Bronze Age. To enter the circle you must clamber through a split tree with a Y-shaped fork. Inside, the world turns on its head: the mighty oak exposes its roots to the air and grows into the earth; all the posts are positioned with their bark facing outwards, apart from one. Holme is a sandy beach now, but originally this area was salt marsh. A liminal, watery place where upturned trees formed a secret circle. What happened on the altar of the oak stump? Dead bodies laid out, sacrifices made, offerings burned? The circle keeps its secrets. Seahenge is now on display in Lynn Museum, King's Lynn.

Saltfleetby Spindle Whorl

Viking magic written in runes

Lincolnshire

Left An everyday object with a secret message. This spindle whorl is covered in runes that ask for the help of the old Norse gods.

This little lump of lead with a hole in the middle reveals a puzzling yet universal human truth – that people can comfortably think two incompatible things at once. It's a spindle whorl – a weight that helps pull a bundle of wool downwards and twist it into yarn during hand-spinning. That yarn can then be woven into cloth. In order to make enough yarn to produce a typical set of medieval adult's clothes you'd need the wool of up to six sheep, spun into 40 km (25 miles) of yarn. The spinning, weaving and sewing would take weeks of hard, skilled work.

Until its industrialisation in the 1770s, all spinning was done by hand, mostly in the home. We find spindle whorls on British archaeological sites from the Bronze Age to the 1500s. They can be made of stone, clay, bone, wood and lead, and the weight of the whorl determines the thickness of the yarn – the lighter the weight, the finer the yarn. Because they're solid, chunky items, spindle whorls tend to survive quite well in archaeological contexts. This one, from the early eleventh century, is made from lead and weighs 50 g (1¾ oz), which is about middle-weight for a whorl. It survived life in a ploughed field for hundreds of years before it was discovered by a metal detectorist in 2010.

What makes it a rare treasure is its inscription: it's covered with Viking runes. Only half the runes are legible, and they've had the experts in contortions. The inscription starts on the vertical wall, and continues on the upper face. Firstly, *.open.ok.einmtalr.ok.palfa.peir.*, which can be translated as 'Odin and Heimdallr and Thjalfa, they . . .'

Odin is the chief of the Norse gods and represents wisdom, battle, honour and magic. In Saxon traditions, Odin is equivalent to Woden, and lends his name to the middle of the week – Woden's Day (Wednesday). Frigg, his wife, has Friday. Heimdallr is also a Norse god, and lives as a watchman at the edge of the realm of the gods with a golden-maned horse, nine mothers and a horn that can be heard in heaven, earth and

63

Below Runic inscriptions are more common in Britain than you might expect. More than thirty inscriptions have been found inside the prehistoric tomb of Maeshowe on Orkney. They say, among other things, 'Haermund Hardaxe carved these runes' and 'Ingigerth is the most beautiful of all women.' Some themes in graffiti never change.

the lower world. He's said to be able to hear the grass grow, can see a hundred leagues and needs less sleep than a bird.

'Thjalfa' is puzzling – it could be linked to the human servant-boy in the Norse sagas, Thajalfi, but this would be a female version of the name, which isn't known anywhere else in Norse inscriptions or stories. It might also be an unusual, poetic word for the sea.

On the upper face of the whorl the inscription continues: *ielba. peruolflt.ok.kiriuesf.*, which means '. . . help you Úlfljótr and . . .' Úlfljótr is a man's name. The last legible word, *kiriuesf*, is a total mystery, and so is the rest of the inscription.

So in total, what we can read says 'Odin and Heimdallr and Thjalfa, will help you, Úlfljótr and . . .' It sounds like a prayer. The Norse colonists in this part of coastal Lincolnshire had been around for some four to six generations by the early eleventh century. They weren't raiding and

pillaging, they were farming and building and getting on with their settled, mostly peaceful lives. They had local styles of tools and trappings, but they also stayed connected to the old country, culturally and linguistically. The inscription on this whorl, for example, demonstrates cutting-edge innovations in runic grammar.

But however impressive the Lincolnshire Vikings' literacy was, why inscribe a plea to the gods onto a spindle whorl in the first place? Because spinning was not just a necessary and slightly tedious domestic task: in Old Norse literature, spinning and weaving are regularly associated with fate and magic. Women in the stories weave shirts that protect their menfolk in battle; others weave poisoned shirts that bring death and misfortune. The three goddesses of fate, the Norns, represent past, present and future, and are said to spin the threads of life itself, deciding the fate of all living beings. When a baby is born, the Norns are always near by and through their spinning, they create a web that binds us inextricably into one another's lives. The mystical power of spinning and weaving can be seen beyond the Viking world too. Threads and cords are frequently worn or woven into protective charms in many world cultures, including Hinduism, Native American traditions and kabbalistic Judaism. In Britain, too, we retain traditions of protective textiles – christening gowns and bridal garters being just two examples.

Other Viking spindle whorls have been found carved from rock crystal, amber and jet, potent materials that would have had more than just a functional purpose. As a spindle whorl turned, catching the light and twisting the fibres, it could harness magic from goddesses like Frigg. If a woman spun well, she could weave protection into every fibre of her family's clothes. Perhaps this was the purpose of the inscription on the Saltfleetby spindle whorl. But – and this is the fascinating thing – by the eleventh century the ethnically Norse people of Lincolnshire were Christian. They built churches to St Clement, a patron saint of seafarers, they were buried in Christian graveyards. By all accounts, they weren't worshipping the pantheon of old Gods, they had one, new, everlasting God who didn't tolerate the worship of false idols. But people can hold all manner of conflicting beliefs in their minds at once, especially when dealing with something as important as the safety of their loved ones. Perhaps that's why a Christian Viking scratched a prayer to the old gods on the sides of this spindle whorl: because they loved their family.

Snettisham Treasures

Golden hoards buried by Boudicca's ancestors

Norfolk

Left Pits at Snettisham have yielded over 40 kg (88 lb) of gold, silver and bronze, including two hundred neck rings known as 'torcs'. These may have been the Iron Age equivalent of a crown.

The Snettisham treasures are the greatest collection of Iron Age items ever discovered in Britain and yet they guard their secrets close. Like many of the great archaeological discoveries, this one was found by accident. In 1948 a ploughman was working more deeply than usual, and turned up what his foreman thought was a brass bedstead. More bits of 'brass' appeared and it turned out that the bedstead was actually the terminal of a solid gold torc – a type of neck ornament worn in the late Bronze Age and Iron Age (around 1300 BC until the time around the Roman invasion in AD 43).

Archaeologists at Norwich Museum discovered and excavated a series of pits, each contained a hoard of treasure. Then more items were turned up during ploughing in the 1950s, 1960s and 1970s: coins, ingots and pieces of jewellery. Surely that was everything? In the 1990s, powerful new metal detectors became widely available. One detectorist discovered a bronze box full of Iron Age metal fragments. The authorities realised that this strange field needed to be thoroughly investigated again. Six more hoards were uncovered – not scrap fragments waiting to be recycled, but so-called 'repository hoards' – pristine items carefully collected and buried together.

Each pit appeared to be relatively shallow. Then, when the excavators trowelled down, they discovered another, secret pit, dug directly under the first. Unfailingly, this lower pit was filled with even more valuable treasures. It appears that the upper chambers were, in fact, decoy pits, concealing the real valuables beneath. The biggest collection of treasure was Hoard L. It contained seven bronze and silver torcs on the upper level pit, and, in the 'secret' pit, an astonishing ten gold torcs, two silver torcs and two bronze bracelets.

The so-called Great Torc is a marvel of artistry. It's made from more than 1 kg (2 lb 3 oz) of pure gold mixed with pure silver. Tiny twisted gold threads have been teased into eight bundles of eight, and then wrapped round each other to make one majestic rope. The terminals are hollow

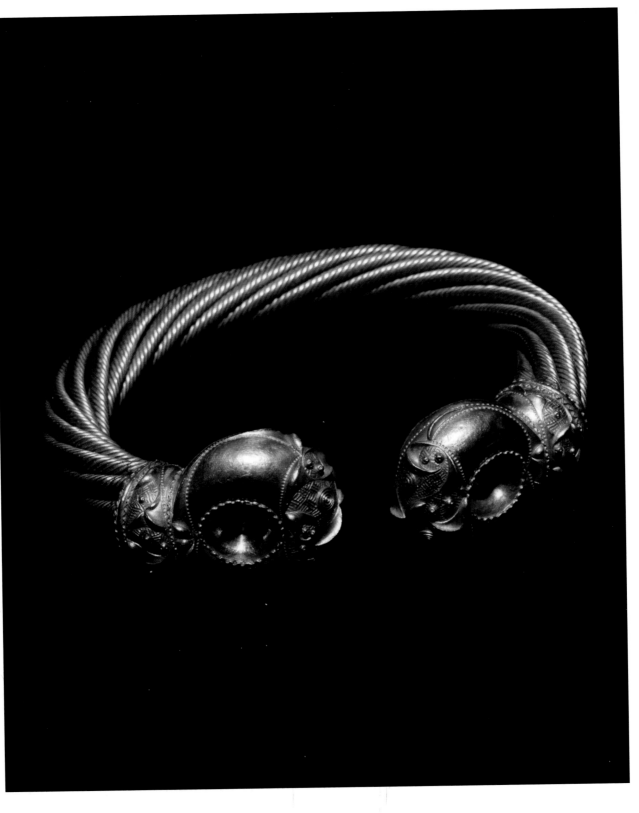

pieces cast in a mould, then welded on. The treasures in the pits represent the pinnacle of Celtic craftsmanship from the pre-Roman period. The artwork styles suggest that they were all created between 100 and 60 BC.

Who buried 40 kg (88 lb) of gold, bronze and silver, including 200 torcs? These were rare and precious artefacts, the Iron Age equivalent of a diamond necklace or even a crown. Are these gifts to the gods, or were they valuables buried for safekeeping? Was it all done in one go, or do the Snettisham pits represent many years of deposits? And why did the people not return to reclaim this treasure?

One interpretation is that the Snettisham treasures were the valuables of wealthy tribal households fleeing the first Roman invasion of Britain in 55 BC. Amid such fear and uncertainty, perhaps the safest thing to do would be to bury your gold and head for the hills. The people who didn't make it back didn't get a chance to retrieve their valuables.

Some of the jewellery would have been almost fifty years old when it was buried, which makes sense; items as precious as these would have been treasured for generations. But the coins found in the hoards confound the refugee theory. Most of the coins were minted on the continent, around 70 BC, and would have made their way to Norfolk through trade and exchange. If the hoards had been hidden during Caesar's invasion in 55 BC, we'd expect to see coins that were minted in the 50s as well as earlier. The range of coins suggests that the deposits were actually made some years before the Romans darkened the doorstep.

The second explanation is that these objects were ritual offerings, deposited into the ground for the gods, or spirits. People never intended to dig them up again. It gives us an idea about just how rich these people must have been, that they could afford to dispose of such wealth.

The people who ruled this area in the first century BC were the Iceni. They're perhaps best known for the later Iceni queen Boudicca, who revolted against Roman rule in AD 60/61, and destroyed the Roman towns of Colchester, London and St Albans before being defeated. But in the century before, evidence suggests that the Iceni were part of a loose federation of smaller tribal groups who surrendered to the Romans in 54 BC. Their wealth was built on agriculture – grain, livestock and maybe wool, and they perhaps decided it would be a better plan to do a deal with potentially good customers, rather than stand and fight.

We don't know whether these torcs were secret offerings in a sacred grove, or whether they were events for the whole community to witness and celebrate. Were they celebratory – deposits made at important births or marriage unions or to help the deceased achieve the afterlife? Or perhaps these beautiful artefacts were consigned to the earth when something went wrong; a lost battle with a neighbouring tribe or in the aftermath of a failed harvest. The treasures have been unearthed, but their secrets have not.

Must Farm

The Pompeii of the Fens

Cambridgeshire

Left The level of organic preservation at Must Farm is mind-blowing. This wooden wheel is more than 3,000 years old, and was probably used in a two-wheeled cart drawn by oxen.

The first pieces of shaped timber were spotted sticking out of the side of the Cambridgeshire quarry in 1999, and in 2015, archaeologists finally got to excavate this magical Bronze Age site thoroughly. Must Farm is a lost stilt village from around 900 BC that was destroyed in a catastrophic fire, which made the houses collapse with all their contents trapped inside. It's an archaeological time capsule – a thrilling cross between the *Marie Celeste* and Pompeii.

About half the site was lost to quarrying in the 1900s but the half we do have is packed with treasures. Incredibly, because the ground is waterlogged, all the organic materials have been preserved, even though they're 3,000 years old. There are buckets, baskets and pottery bowls with wooden spoons and half-eaten meals inside them (wheat and barley stew with nettles, anyone?). Tools and weapons still have their wooden handles. The five buildings – four roundhouses and a possible rectangular entrance house – were preserved where they fell, with the upright posts *in situ*. It means we know how they were built – on raised frames above a marshy river channel, with woven wattle floors and thatched roofs with radiating rafters. Inside there were separate areas for cooking and craft, and the houses had farming tools like sickles as well as stored seed grain and weapons – bronze swords and spears particularly. The houses were attached to each other and to the drier, higher land, by wattle walkways. And in the river channel there were large sturdy log boats. They're carved from huge individual tree trunks, with end plates to keep the water out. In the hands of a skilled paddler, you'd be able to undertake quite significant journeys in them along the rivers and around the coast.

Radiocarbon dating shows the trees used to make the outer fence and house posts were felled between 1000 and 900 BC. Many of them retain their bark and sapwood, which means the timber was fresh, or 'green', rather than seasoned when it was used. There's no evidence for wood-

Above Intact pottery vessels still contain uneaten food.

boring insect damage in the timbers, and there's hardly any silt build up between the woodchips from construction and the fire 'destruction horizon'. From this, we can deduce that the village must have burned down shortly after it was built.

Was the fire a terrible accident or were the people of Must Farm attacked? Fires would have been a relatively common occurrence in a time when open flames were used for cooking, lighting and heating, and everything around you was made of combustible materials. There isn't evidence for any human victims of the fire, so if it was an accidental fire and the people escaped, you might expect them to come back and rebuild, or try and retrieve some of their possessions. If this was an arson attack by a neighbouring tribe, why didn't the Must Farm people pick up their swords, spears and axes as they escaped? These were not just tools to defend yourself, but also valuable items that would be expensive or impossible to replace. Perhaps the residents had already been killed or chased away, and the burning of the village happened after its hurried abandonment. Whatever it was, the eerie presence of every possession suggests something catastrophic.

Although we don't know what happened to the residents of Must Farm, we can build a remarkable picture of their lives. Discarded animal bones showed they were hunters as well as farmers; there was wild boar and red deer, as well as mutton, veal and pork. They grew and milled grains like wheat and barley and enjoyed porridge, stews and roast dinners. They had lots of stuff in their houses, both functional and beautiful, including sets of nested pottery vessels, delicate drinking cups and wooden platters. Textiles were made from flax and nettle fibres, wool, cow and horse hair. Some of the linen is so fine it would meet the requirements for modern couture clothing. And more than eighty beads were recovered, made from Baltic amber, Whitby jet and glass produced in the Mediterranean or Middle East. The Must Farmers also kept lambs in their houses – evidenced both from the droppings everywhere, and from the complete skeletons found indoors, which may be animals that fell victim to the fire.

The environmental conditions at Must Farm mean that even the least fancy of archaeological samples has been preserved – poo. Analysis of the human and canine coprolites shows that the dogs were eating the same food as the humans (probably table scraps – some things never change). But the human poo is intriguing. It shows people were eating freshwater proteins and were infected with intestinal parasites that you'd get from things like fish, shellfish and frogs if you don't cook them thoroughly. That said, there isn't much other evidence of them eating river food – no piles of discarded mussel shells, for example.

Analysing the isotopes of various chemical elements laid down in your teeth and bones can indicate what kind of food you've eaten over the long term. From the few pieces of human bone that were found, the isotope signatures indicate the people had grown up eating terrestrial resources – milk and meat – rather than fish. So had these Must Farm people recently shifted to eating more fish? Is this linked to their new home above the river? If so, where did they live before? We don't yet know.

What we do know is that these people were farmers, but they also used boats to get around and thought living on the river was a good idea. They were settled here, with all their things, and with animals and crops stored for the coming year. They produced enough surplus to trade for rare jewellery and fancy goods. Yet all this wasn't enough to save them from disaster – perhaps their wealth was the reason neighbours or raiders turned on them. Or perhaps it was because they were newly arrived immigrants. We often think of the past as static or slow moving, but this extraordinary site captures how radically life can change, from one tumultuous day to the next.

Below The timber-framed roundhouses were preserved where they collapsed, with the vertical posts still *in situ*. These houses stood on stilts above a small river channel, and were linked to one another by woven wattle walkways.

Baldehildis Seal

A queen's lost ring

Norfolk

Above Just 12 mm (½ in) across, this solid, 98 per cent pure gold disc dates from around AD 600–700 and was found by a metal detectorist in a field in Norfolk. It was designed to be attached to a finger ring, and it swivels on the central pin so both sides can be used for stamping imprints into wax seals. On one side is the engraved image of a woman with flowing hair, and letters spelling the female name 'Baldehildis'. On the side shown are two figures under a Christian cross: a long-haired woman and a bearded man. They appear to be naked and possibly having sexual intercourse. The most likely owner of this gold seal ring is Queen Balthild, who grew up in a royal household in East Anglia and married the Frankish King Clovis II in AD 648. It's possible this seal was commissioned to mark their union at a time when elite women were well-educated and respected enough to be sending letters and documents under their own seals. How her ring was lost we can only guess at.

Colchester Face Pot

A spirited Roman cremation vessel

Essex

Above This urn was used to hold the cremated remains of a Roman, probably a soldier involved in the successful invasion of Britain in AD 43. It was discovered in Colchester, or Camulodunum as he would have known it, the first Roman capital of Britain.

These face pots are particularly associated with soldiers in the Roman army, and seem to have been popular in Britain. The face on the pot might have been intended to look like the deceased person, or perhaps it represents a spirit tasked with the safe-keeping of the remains.

Camulodunum was destroyed when the native Iceni leader Queen Boudicca revolted in AD 60/61, burning the city and massacring its citizens. She continued on to destroy London and St Albans before being defeated by Roman troops. We don't know exactly where the battle took place, or whether Boudicca was killed in the fight, died later of wounds or escaped. Her whereabouts remain unknown.

Grimes Graves

*400 pits from
Neolithic flint mining*

Norfolk

Right This bizarre, pock-marked landscape is the result of flint mining from some 4,500 years ago. Miners dug shafts 13 m (43 ft) deep with deer antler picks, and then extended horizontal galleries outwards to reach the desirable black 'floorstone' flint to make prestigious blades and tools. This wasn't just an industrial place, it was a magical place: chalk effigies of cups, balls and penises have been found in the mines, along with pottery, stone axes and animal remains. Were these offerings to keep miners safe, to thank the earth or the gods for the flint, or a place to reach beyond this realm? A mine is a powerful place – a man-made underworld, where the veil between realms is perhaps thinner.

Dunwich

Britain's medieval Atlantis

Suffolk

Left The standing remains of the Greyfriars Franciscan monastery on the west side of the medieval town. In 1538 the friary was suppressed as part of the Dissolution of the Monasteries, and converted into a secular house. Much of the monastic archaeology survives, but like the rest of medieval Dunwich, stands at risk of falling into the sea.

Dunwich is a sleepy village of 120 souls on the Suffolk coast. It's also Britain's Atlantis.

In the eleventh century it was – and this is hard to believe – an internationally important port, and one of the biggest urban settlements in the country. It started life in the Iron Age and by Saxon times it boasted numerous churches and a vast town boundary, known as Pales Dyke. Excavation has shown it was a ditch more than 12 m (39 ft) wide and 4.5 m (15 ft) deep, with a bank and palisade fence on top – defendable but also an impressive status symbol. By the time the Domesday Book was being compiled, Dunwich boasted a population of 3,000. The Normans could see the strategic importance of a place like this. It had everything – good navigation into the North Sea and a safe harbour. The town served as a naval base and an embarkation point for crusaders beginning their journeys to the Holy Land. They had a shipbuilding industry and a seventy vessel fishing fleet. There was a Greyfriars monastery, a Blackfriars monastery, a hospital for pilgrims, windmills, taverns, tollgates and a sizeable marketplace. Dunwich was the real deal.

But then the storms came. On New Year's Day 1286, a three-day storm began. Seawater surged through the town, buildings were destroyed, people and animals drowned. When the clouds finally lifted, the residents found the coastline had transformed and the river now emptied into the sea an incredible 3.2 km (2 miles) away.

Working in treacherous conditions, the people of Dunwich tried to restore the shipping channels and rebuild their harbour. But then two months later, the storm surges happened again. And then again, the next winter. The economy declined, so too did the population. More epic storms in 1326, 1328 and 1338 sealed the fate of Britain's lost city. Hundreds of homes were swept into the sea, the navigable boat channels were lost and eight churches had gone.

If you stand on the beach today, in front of you, under the waves, are the remains of the lost town still laid out in a frozen street plan. Romantics say that some days you'll hear the sound of drowned church bells on the wind. The water isn't deep – just 3 m (10 ft) in some parts – but the silt means visibility is close to zero. Archaeologists have used acoustic imaging to record the ruins, and confirm the extent of the once-thriving medieval metropolis.

What remains gives just a hint of what has been lost. There are a few houses, a seventeenth-century pub, the chapel of St James' leper hospital and the ruins of Greyfriars monastery teetering high on the cliff. But the inexorable march of the sea continues – the remaining gravestones and burials in All Saints' churchyard are predicted to be lost within the next fifteen to twenty years. The battle against coastal erosion continues, but Dunwich will drown eventually.

Wenhaston Doom Painting

A vision of hell

Suffolk

Right In 1892 it was decided Wenhaston village church deserved a new chancel arch. The whitewashed planks of the old arch were dumped in the churchyard and left overnight. When the labourers returned the next morning to finish their work, they saw the rain had washed off the white to reveal painted images beneath – an extraordinary medieval depiction of the Last Judgement, or Doom, when every soul is measured to be worthy of salvation, or condemned to Hell for eternity. On the left side, the worthy enter Heaven. On the right, damned souls are drawn into Hell by demons with red-hot chains and grappling hooks. The fanged Hell's Mouth is strikingly similar to the demon under the pentangle in Troston (page 83). Parishioners gazing at this screen didn't see art, they saw a warning. The suffering of this world was nothing compared to the possible fate of your eternal soul after death. Sinners beware.

Troston Demon

Evil pinned down on a church wall

Suffolk

Left A demon, pinned down by a pentangle that's been scored over and over again by medieval parishioners.

The east face of the chancel arch, nearest the altar, in St Mary's Church, Troston, in Suffolk, is covered in graffiti. It's not recent – the parishioners who carved it were medieval. And this graffiti is not antisocial; they're words and drawings probably better regarded as a form of sacred art. There are human figures with their arms raised in prayer, crosses, Latin inscriptions, personal names and symbols of the ragged staff, which is usually associated with St Christopher. They're jumbled over one another, representing hundreds of years of parish life and the prayers, memorials and marks of grief and thanks of local people. And just above the melee is this, the Troston Demon.

The demon is grotesque, with a bulbed nose and pointed ears. Its gaping maw is full of teeth and a massive, lolling tongue. The mouth is reaching out, perhaps to gobble or grab the unwary or sinful soul. Over the top of the demon, scored over its neck, is a five-pointed star, or pentangle. It's been carved deeply, and drawn again and again, people retracing the unbroken line of the pentangle pattern.

The pentangle is an 'apotropaic', or ritual protection mark. In the fourteenth-century story of *Sir Gawain and the Green Knight*, Gawain, one of King Arthur's knights, goes on a quest to meet the mystical Green Knight. His shield is described as shining scarlet with a pentangle of pure gold. This, the anonymous author of the text describes, is a mark of Solomon, and, like the five points of the star, it will protect him in five times five ways. It represents the five wounds of Christ, the five joys of Mary, God's five fingers, the five senses and the five knightly virtues: generosity, courtesy, chastity, chivalry and piety. The pentangle is a powerful and Godly symbol.

In Troston church, the pentangle pins the demon down and neutralises its evil power. Every time someone retraced the shape, it perhaps renewed the protective energy of the pentangle and extended it to the new person. It's not hard to imagine that tracing the line of the sacred star would have become part of local tradition, where everyone who came to make their mark on the church also traced the line of the pentangle, a bit like rubbing the toe/head/nose of a statue for luck.

Carved in the plain stone of the wall and traced over so many times, it's now quite hard to see the original demon. But when it was first drawn, the church walls would have had a coloured plaster on them and the demon and pentangle would have stood out clearly. God was everywhere, and everything. And where there was God, there was also the Devil – and spirits and demons intent on causing trouble and leading people into temptation and sin. If tracing the pentangle might keep your family and home safe, and perhaps even save your soul from the everlasting torments of Hell, why would you *not* make your mark?

Sutton Hoo

The one-eyed king in the mound

Suffolk

Left A bird-like dragon forms the nose, eyebrows and moustache of the helmet and another dragon sits over the helmet's crest. The crest dragon's left eye has no gold behind the garnet. The same is true of the bird dragon's right wing (the left eyebrow). The wearer of the helmet has become a one-eyed God.

Next page The Sutton Hoo burial site was used by the royal Wuffing family, rulers of East Anglia in the sixth, seventh and eighth centuries AD. Many of the earth mounds have been eroded away over the centuries, but traces of the burials remain.

Sutton Hoo is the royal burial ground of the Wuffing family, who ruled the Anglo-Saxon kingdom of East Anglia (modern-day Norfolk and Suffolk) in the sixth, seventh and eighth centuries AD. Their palace was at Rendlesham and, just 6.4 km (4 miles) downstream on a bend in the River Deben, a great field of earthen barrows was constructed to mark the resting places of their most celebrated people, including wealthy women – perhaps queens or princesses – and warriors buried with their horses. These people's names are now lost to history. Over the centuries, grave-robbers targeted some of the mounds, destroying the archaeological remains in the process. But they didn't attack the biggest, Mound 1. It was first excavated in 1939, and the archaeologists made an astonishing discovery. It was a ship burial – literally, a body laid to rest in a whole ship that had then been covered over with earth. We'll never be 100 per cent certain, but it's pretty much agreed that this Great Ship Burial is King Raedwald, who died in AD 625.

The excavators found no surviving wood from the 27-m (90-ft) ship, and no remains of the body, as all the organic materials had rotted away in the acidic sandy soil. But the ship's timbers had stained the soil, and the archaeologists were able to build a perfect 3D plan from the positions of the hundreds of rusted iron rivets that had held the vessel together. Recent analysis of the soil phosphate levels has confirmed that the centre of the ship had indeed held a body. Raedwald had been placed in a wooden chamber in the ship's hull and surrounded with important possessions that he'd need in the next life. In death, as in life, he looked like a king and the treasures in his grave represent the impressive wealth and reach of British rulers in the so-called Dark Ages.

Raedwald wore gold-and-garnet shoulder clasps that harked back to the days of the Roman Emperors, and a great gold belt buckle with a hollow section in its body that might have served as a secret

Above The perfectly carved fine-grained whetstone has distinctive, detailed faces on each end, perhaps representing gods or ancestors. A bronze stag stands at the top, fixed to an iron ring. It's likely this is a ceremonial sceptre, declaring the king's nobility, bravery and ability to defend his people.

compartment for a sacred relic. He had a pattern-welded iron sword decorated with garnets from Sri Lanka. His vast shield was probably a gift from allies in Scandinavia. He had tableware from Byzantium (modern-day Turkey), and drinking horns, bowls, buckets and cauldrons, which were used to host feasts that bonded his kinsmen and demonstrated his generosity. He had a lyre for music and poetry, and a pair of silver spoons with Greek inscriptions.

Perhaps the most enigmatic item in the ship burial is a carved and decorated four-sided stone bar. It might be a sceptre, or it could be a ceremonial version of a whetstone used to sharpen swords. It's 50 cm (20 in) long, and made from a dense, fine-grained stone called greywacke that's not found in Suffolk. The central section is pristine (which means it hasn't been used to sharpen anything) and is entirely plain. In the Anglo-Saxon period, when every available surface of a high-status object would be elaborately decorated, this expanse of plain stone is striking. On each face of each end of the bar, there are intricately carved human faces. Each has distinct facial hair and features that might suggest they represent particular individuals, perhaps ancestors or gods. At the (assumed) base, there's a small bronze cup shape, and at the other end, a large iron ring supporting a finely-wrought bronze stag sculpture. It's difficult to hold, and it doesn't easily stand up on its own, but this sceptre-whetstone was clearly hugely important, perhaps indicating the King as the ever-ready protector of his realm.

And then there's the famous helmet. Made from tin, silver, iron, bronze, gold and garnets, it's one of the finest pieces of workmanship from medieval Europe. Panels around the head have an animal interlace and two repeating warrior motifs. One shows horned warriors engaged in a ritual dance with spears and swords. The other is of a warrior being trampled under his adversary's horse just at the moment he's driving a sword into the animal's chest. The crest over the crown of the head is formed by a serpent-like dragon, with a head at each end, and the nose and brow of the helmet are in the form of a bird-like dragon, wings outstretched to form the eyebrows, its tail forming the moustache.

Every piece of gold and garnet work on every item in the ship burial has gold foil behind it, except two: under an eyebrow of the helmet and under one of the crest dragon's eyes. The row of garnets forming the right eyebrow has foil, the row along the left eyebrow does not. Similarly, the left eye of the dragon has no foil. Without the foil, the garnets are darker, and instead of sparkling, they seem to absorb the light. Was this human error? Hardly. Craftspeople working at this level wouldn't make such obvious mistakes. And to make two left-eye mistakes is unthinkable. And the strange theme continues: when an expert was creating an exact replica of the sceptre-whetstone for the site's museum, he noticed that a left eye on one of the eight faces had been carved to be symmetrical, and then chipped out with a chisel. The whetstone is made from incredibly hard stone, which means that it can't have been a moment of clumsiness. It was careful and deliberate.

The most compelling explanation is that all these damaged eyes are demonstrations of Raedwald's relationship with Woden, the chief of the old gods and the greatest warrior, who traded his left eye in exchange for wisdom. The tradition of the one-eyed god is very ancient indeed, perhaps prehistoric in origin, as evidenced by the 3,000 year old Dagenham Idol (page 102). It's even possible that Raedwald in his helmet was considered to be a living embodiment of Woden himself.

We're not sure if Raedwald considered himself Christian when he died, but he was definitely aware of the power of the new faith. The monk Bede wrote a history in the 700s AD, and says Raedwald was baptised when he visited the neighbouring kingdom of Kent in AD 604 (perhaps attending St Martin's chapel, page 107). But when he returned to his people, his Queen was enraged. Their strength as leaders was based on fealty – and a new god might destabilise those relationships. So Raedwald attempted to keep everyone happy by erecting a Christian altar in the temple next to the pagan one. It quickly came to be known as 'The Temple with Two Altars'. Raedwald was a diplomat and a warrior. He was a baptised king, but he dressed as Woden. He lived and died at one of the most remarkable times in British history, and through this extraordinary grave, we can peek into his world.

Below This clasp would have attached to a leather purse hanging at the King's waist. The central motifs show birds of prey on the backs of duck-like birds. Either side is an enigmatic 'Master of Animals' image, with a man between two pouncing wolves. Is he being attacked, or is he subduing them?

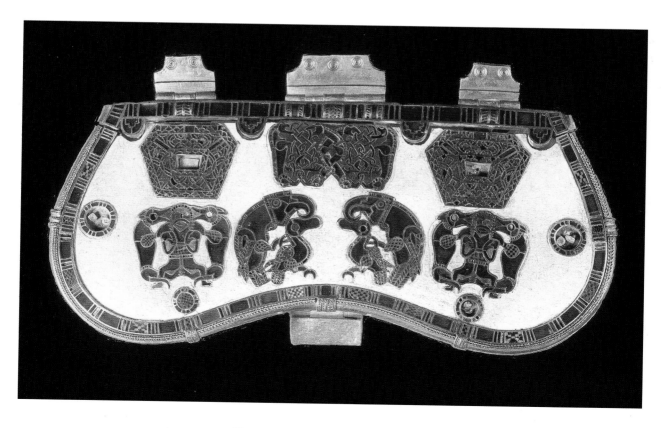

Greensted Church

The oldest wooden church in the world

Essex

From over the hedge, you could be forgiven for mistaking Greensted church for a domestic house. But in fact, it's the oldest wooden church in the world. And on the site of this ancient building, pagans and Christians have fought the ultimate battle for faith.

The earliest evidence for a church on this spot is from the 650s AD, when St Cedd, a monk sent from the Northumbrian island of Lindisfarne, was invited to begin converting the East Saxon people, who still give their name to the county, Essex. Previous attempts to convert the kings of Essex had only ever been temporarily successful, and were swiftly followed by a pagan resurgence. The same thing happened again and again; King Sigeberht converted during Cedd's mission and was then murdered, apparently for being too forgiving of his enemies. His death in AD 660 led to another swing towards paganism under King Swithhelm. Then back to Christianity, when Swithhelm converted in AD 662. And then back to paganism when he died in AD 664 and plague broke out in AD 665, provoking his cousin Sighere to abandon 'the mysteries of the Christian faith' (according to Bede) and lead his half of the Kingdom back to the old gods. Essex remained part-Christian, part-pagan for another twenty years, until Sighere died and Sebbi, his devout cousin, took over the whole kingdom and extended his faith to all of Essex, as well as founding the original abbey at Westminster.

We don't know what happened here on the site of St Andrew's as the old gods and new gods battled through the seventh century, but enough survived in order for the site to retain its identity as a place of worship. Of what we see today, the nave – the main body of the church – dates to the next phase of building in 1053. Fifty-one of the original oak wall timbers survive – they were rammed into the earth, end-on, side by side, to form a solid wall, known as a palisade. A thousand years later they're still standing strong.

You can still see the tool marks made by medieval woodsmen on these venerable timbers. Darkened patches visible inside the church may be where oil lamps were burned. The chancel, the area around the altar, was rebuilt in brick in the 1500s, at the same time the dormer windows in the roof were added. These types of window are more usually found in domestic houses, and churches would normally have added what's known as a clerestory, by rebuilding the walls with a row of windows near the roof line (a 'clear storey'). If that decision had been made at Greensted, the nave would have been rebuilt in stone and the oldest wooden church in the world would have been put on a bonfire. Whether it was the work of the Christian God, pagan gods, or simply fate, Greensted church still stands today.

Left The choice to insert quirky dormer windows in the roof secured this ancient timber church's survival. The black timbers to the right of the tower were erected in AD 1053.

Guildhall Witch Bottle

A hidden cure for witchcraft

London

Right Bellarmine jugs were popular choices for making seventeenth-century witch bottles. They were easy to obtain, but maybe the body and face added to their counter-magical appeal.

This seventeenth-century stoneware bottle known as a bellarmine, or Bartmann (literally 'bearded man') jug, was found hidden in the surviving foundations of a brick cellar under a building that was otherwise destroyed in the Great Fire of London, in 1666.

It's a witch bottle: not something that contains a witch – but a tool to protect you from witches, or cure you from bewitchment, if you've already been affected. Hundreds of witch bottles have been recorded in Britain, and the 'recipe' appears very odd but surprisingly consistent: a mixture of sharp, bent metal items like pins, and human urine. Most contain some extras too, like nail clippings, hair and pieces of leather or cloth. A concealed bellarmine found in Greenwich in 2009 contained bent iron nails, brass pins, a heart-shaped piece of leather, human hair, nail clippings and belly button fluff, all soaked in human urine. We don't know the details of this counter-magical thinking, but it seems possible that proponents of this cure might suggest the bodily elements would draw the evil to the bottle, entangle it, then the bent nails would pin it down and drown it in the urine.

Intriguingly, the Guildhall Yard bottle is a little different. Its contents had been pushed into the bottle, then set alight. The surviving bubbly, carbonised layer doesn't contain any traces of the usual metal artefacts and we can't tell if it contained wee. Frustratingly, we don't know the exact circumstances in which this bottle was buried, or why the creator used a different 'cure' to normal.

New research suggests that witch bottles weren't usually created in response to fears about a particular witch, but were 'off the shelf' cures for the more general ailment of bewitchment. If you feared you'd been afflicted – having nightmares, suffering great fatigue, depression, seizures or fainting for example – you could approach an astrologer-physician, apothecary, or 'cunning' man or woman (a folk healer who often treated poorer people) and they would prepare a cure for you.

Bellarmines were particularly popular as witch bottles. They were mass-produced in Germany as containers for wine and gin, so some of their frequency can be explained in that they were easy to get hold of and preserve well. But maybe the big beardy face and bulbous belly of the jug appealed; perhaps the vessel itself contributed an animated essence.

The seventeenth century was the peak period for witch bottle-making, when healing was as much about faith as it was about early modern 'science'. But witch bottles have been discovered dating to Victorian times, and in 1988 a plastic medicine bottle was found in the River Thames containing a halfpenny, a dime, human teeth, a wrapped piece of metal and a small vial of clove oil. It's easy to dismiss these artefacts as superstition. But we still seek ways to explain sudden changes in fortune. Why did you win the lottery? Why did that cell become cancerous? We might be able to explain the physiological process of a disease in objective terms, but we can't explain *why* any better than our forebears.

Flag Fen

The power and pull of water spirits

Cambridgeshire

Some time between 1365 and 967 BC, the Bronze Age residents of Peterborough took time out from raising sheep and cattle, planting and harvesting crops and creating fine bronze swords, axeheads and jewellery, to gather more than 60,000 pieces of timber to make a 5 m (16 ft) wide, 1,000 m (3,280 ft) long wooden causeway over a low, marshy landscape. It doesn't obviously lead to or from, anywhere.

How do we know this? The waterlogged land near Peterborough has preserved traces of our ancestors' activities dating back some 3,000 years. Normally, organic material like wood will rot away quite quickly. But if it's in an environment very low in oxygen, then the microbes that normally decompose stuff, can't. Peat bogs, where the water is acidic and deoxygenated, are perfect preservers. That's why we get bog bodies (page 203), bog butter (literally vats of prehistoric butter found in their original wooden containers, preserved in peat), the remains of Must Farm (page 71) and the causeways of Flag Fen.

The clue that reveals this wasn't just a walkway built to prevent farmers getting their feet wet, is that hundreds of precious items were carefully placed into the watery land either side of it. Some of the swords and daggers had been 'killed' – broken in half or bent in two. We don't know if it's because they were made as an offering to the gods, or whether they were disposed of in a ceremonial way when, for example, their original owners died. Was it bad luck to keep a dead man's sword? Did the gods needed paying, or placating? Or was throwing something as valuable as a sword into a lake a public demonstration of wealth and power – only a few individuals could afford to dispose of such treasures.

Throughout the Bronze and Iron Ages, people across Britain performed rituals around the water. Sacred places were where water and land met, where the distinction between above and below was no longer clear and your senses might not be trusted. Perhaps the veil between the normal and the supernatural was seen as thinner here. It's even been suggested that tales of magical swords thrown into lakes, like King Arthur's Excalibur, have their folk origins in the reality of Bronze Age religious practices like those we see at Flag Fen. And what about dropping a penny into a wishing well? Who or what are we wishing to?

We don't know if our Bronze Age ancestors only made deposits into the marsh in times of trouble, or whether it was a regular act of thanks, or contrition. And we don't know whether such acts were open to all, or channelled through priestly intermediaries. Only 10 per cent of the Flag Fen site has ever been excavated, but ground water levels are now changing and the fen is drying out. If the prehistoric organics are no longer boggy, the decomposing bacteria can get going and the archaeology will be lost. The metals will, of course, survive, but the extraordinarily rich context in which they lie will turn to dust. The mysteries of the water will soon vanish.

Left There are 60,000 pieces of 3,000-year-old timber preserved *in situ* at Flag Fen in a specially built hangar. The ritual deposits either side of the track make this site truly remarkable.

Royston Cave

A Knights Templar secret chapel?

Hertfordshire

There is an ancient crossroads in Royston, where the Roman road between London and York crosses the prehistoric east–west route of the Icknield Way. Rather surprisingly, in Roman and Saxon times there doesn't appear to be much evidence of activity around the crossroads. But at some point a Christian roadside cross was erected, and in the 1160s a priory for Augustinian monks was established. King Richard I, the Lionheart, awarded the town the right to hold a market in 1189, and things grew from there.

In August 1742, workmen were digging in the market just next to the crossroads and found a millstone buried in the earth. They prised it up to reveal a deep, dark vertical hole. It was narrow, and they couldn't discern what was below. So they did what anyone would do – they tied a small boy to a rope, gave him a candle and lowered him in. What he saw was a curving man-made vault cut from the natural chalk bedrock, filled with soil and debris. The men thought they might have struck treasure – or perhaps an entrance to a network of tunnels that would lead to treasure – so they wasted no time in enlarging the hole and emptying out the debris. They didn't find treasure or tunnels, but they were confronted by a place that still eludes explanation.

The cave is a bottle-shaped cavern, with steep sides and a circular floor. Covering the curved white walls are images – of men, women, hearts, crosses and swords. Little faces peer at you from all directions. Some look familiar, some disconcertingly alien. They're higgledy-piggledy across the walls and not all to the same scale. They're also crude enough to suggest that the carvings are not the work of professionals. It feels intimate, and spooky, at the same time.

Most of the images are Christian. There are two crucifixion scenes, and a large (possibly God-like) hand releasing a dove. There's a

Above This crowned figure might represent King David in the Biblical Psalm 69, in which he cries for God's mercy from numerous enemies. The psalm was particularly treasured by Templars.

large St Christopher on the north side, and a St Catherine holding the symbolic Catherine Wheel. St Lawrence holds a gridiron (associated with his martyrdom) and a figure that might be St George points a sword upwards to a row of thirteen figures. The figures may be Jesus and his disciples, but it's hard to be sure. There's a large figure of a different man holding his arms aloft, and another who may be a king, possibly the crusader Richard the Lionheart, with a queen who may be his bride Berengaria. There are also images of hearts drawn on hands, and hearts within hearts. They seem strangely modern, like something a teenager would doodle on a school textbook. There are a couple of distinctly non-Christian images too, possibly fertility images, including a sheela na gig exposing herself (page 181) and a horse with large genitalia.

On the eastern side of the floor is a shallow depression that's been nicknamed 'the grave'. A human skull was said to have been recovered by the workmen, but we don't know where it is now, and there's no archaeological evidence that suggests 'the grave' was ever used for burial. In fact, there's no archaeological evidence that helps us identify any kind of use whatsoever.

There are no records mentioning the cave before its rediscovery in 1742. There are no folk tales, local myths or obscure clues in place names or property deeds. The cave is totally absent from the collective imagination. It's now accessed through a tunnel which was dug in 1790 by an enterprising local to allow visitors easier access to the cave. The original vertical entrance shaft now sits under the road outside a betting shop. It's likely that in medieval times the road was a little narrower and the cave entrance might have been concealed inside a building or yard.

What is this cave? Who dug it, when and why? There are two main theories. One is that the cave was intentionally and secretly dug to provide a mystical underground sanctum for secret gatherings in the fourteenth or fifteenth centuries. The other is that the cave was originally a chalk quarry pit, which was then reused by a medieval hermit for prayerful isolation. The quarry could possibly be prehistoric, or from around the time Royston priory was being built in the 1100s. A bottle shape is admittedly an unusual shape for quarrying, but there are precedents elsewhere in Hertfordshire for this strange design. Traces of paint on some of the carvings suggest that the images were originally painted. Before the 1530s all Christian churches would have been richly decorated and coloured, so this possibly supports the idea that the cave's users wanted to make the place feel sacred.

If it was a purpose-built secret chamber, the most likely users are the Knights Templar. Theirs was a religious and military order of monks founded in 1119, who dedicated themselves as 'warriors of Christ', protecting soldiers and pilgrims travelling to the Holy Land, and Jerusalem's Holy Temple itself. The Templars took oaths committing themselves to a life of simplicity and sacrifice. Celibacy was expected, and boasting about previous sexual exploits was forbidden. Knightly fashions were rejected, and charity put first. The order took two silent meals a day, were mainly vegetarian and considered both anger and laughter as sinful. But even though individuals practised poverty, as an organisation they were vastly rich and powerful. They owned ships, hundreds of castles and houses and they supported over 7,000 knights, brothers and priests, as well as tens of thousands of officials and laymen stationed between Europe and the Holy Land. They introduced credit and cheque banking systems, and had the indulgence of the Pope.

Below St Catherine holds her symbolic wheel next to Christ on the cross, surrounded by hearts drawn on hands.

Above Concentric rings, an unsheathed sword, and a sheela na gig with her genitalia exposed (page 181).

Partly thanks to modern best-selling fiction and Hollywood movies, the Templars are synonymous with secret rites and global conspiracies about the Holy Grail. Those details aren't true. But they did demand obedience from their members, and performed rituals in secret. It's been suggested that Templar initiation could have been conducted in the cave. It may have had an upper wooden floor, with the earthen floor of the cave below. When initiates first entered the lower level of the cave, they were placed into the grave, perhaps covered in water like a baptism, and they'd emerge clockwise, passing under a large lamp suspended from the ceiling. The idea is that they entered the cave in darkness and ignorance, and then awakened into light and salvation. One carving on the wall may show an initiate – it's a human figure, facing the viewer, holding a candle in one hand and a human skull in the other. Could we be looking at a Templar on the threshold of old and new, moving from spiritual death to rebirth?

Despite their wealth and influence – or perhaps because of it – the Templar Order was destroyed in the early fourteenth century. At the end of the 1200s, Christian crusaders had lost control of the Holy Land to Muslim forces. With their popularity somewhat on the wane, King Philip IV of France, who was deeply in debt to the Templars, took his chance. He alleged that they were heretics, and undertook to bring them to justice (seizing their assets and writing off his debts along the way). On Friday 13 October 1307, he oversaw the co-ordinated arrest of Templars across France. It's believed that this event is the origin of the modern superstition about Friday 13th being unlucky. Under torture, many Templars confessed to denying Christ, spitting on the cross and committing carnal depravity during secret rituals – confessions that would see them burned at the stake. King Philip's agents continued trials against Templars from 1307–12, and hundreds of men were burned alive or died under torture. Those who recanted their false confessions were executed as relapsed heretics. Documents rediscovered in the Vatican archives in 2001 show that the Pope didn't actually think the Templars were guilty of heresy, but decided that the Order should be disbanded anyway, for the good of the Church. His desire to limit the conflict with Philip meant the Templars were doomed.

But although Templars were persecuted to death in France, and their international networks were destroyed, members of the Order in England weren't as harshly treated. King Edward II had only been on the throne for a few months, wasn't a strong ally of King Philip and didn't believe the charges of heresy either. Templars were arrested, but it wasn't a thorough purge, and many brothers were permitted to stay in their religious houses until trial. Torture wasn't used as widely either, so the inquisitors didn't get many confessions. Ultimately, many English members of the Order had a chance to disappear before the authorities came for them. They could have returned to a secular life, or joined a different religious community, keeping their heads down and their vows to themselves. And perhaps this is the origin of Royston Cave: it's a secret spot for veteran Templars to worship together, perhaps even initiate new members into their (literally) underground club. There's certainly one image that appears to venerate a man being burned alive, watched by a multitude. Is this Jacques de Molay, the last Grand Master of the Knights Templar, who was burned at the stake in Paris, in 1314?

There are a number of issues with dating – we can't date the actual chalk cave, so we'll never know if it's prehistoric, medieval or other. The carvings appear to show crowns, swords and clothing details from the 1350s or later – which means if the images were carved by Templars, they would have had to be going strong more than a generation after their apparent extinction. Some scholars have compared the Royston images with carvings discovered at Carlisle Castle in Cumbria, and suggest that they actually date to the 1480s – which would require another five unbroken generations of secret monks to have survived. If it were a hermit living in and carving the cave, either in the 1300s or 1400s, why are there no records of alms or benefactors supporting him? Perhaps it was a short-lived residency that fell from memory. Or he was so solitary, most locals didn't know he was there. There's another date to contend with: carved into a stone in the cave roof is '1347'. But it uses the Arabic numerals 1 3 4 7, rather than Roman numerals, which would have been much more common in 1347. Is this because the writer was familiar with Arabic numeracy from the Holy Lands – perhaps because he was a Templar – or is this a later or doctored detail, added by enterprising folk in the 1700s, looking to deepen the cave's history and increase tourist footfall?

Just 13 km (8 miles) up the road from Royston is the town of Baldock – founded by the Knights Templar in 1140. It's named after a city they loved and knew well, called Baldac – modern-day Baghdad. Deep in the English countryside, evidence of medieval faith and international impact lie hidden in plain sight. Whether the Royston images are a hermit's picture prayers carved in chalk, or the clandestine remains of a condemned order of Knights, the cave is the ultimate enigma.

Dagenham Idol

The 3000-year-old wooden God found in the Thames

Essex

This artefact is made from Scots Pine, is 48 cm (19 in) high and is an astonishing 4,200 years old. You can't mistake its form: a blackened, dish-faced naked figurine, one of the earliest representations of the human form ever discovered in Britain. Its arms are missing, and at its crotch, there's a round hole. Intriguingly, the figure's eyes have been carved to be non-identical. On the right side of its face there's a deep pit, on the left, a smooth dish. This doesn't appear to be a mistake – the idol is one-eyed.

It was discovered by workmen in 1922 while they were digging a trench for sewer pipes for the new Ford Car factory in Dagenham, on the north shores of the River Thames, east of London. It was 3 m (10 ft) down, under a layer of peat, buried next to the skeleton of a deer. Radiocarbon dating shows that the wood it's made from was cut around 2400–2100 BC, at the end of the late Stone Age (also known as the Neolithic) or start of the Bronze Age.

This period is a time when our ancestors were farming, growing crops like barley and rye and raising cattle, sheep and pigs. They lived in small villages of earth and timber huts, and probably worshipped in ways that tried to ensure good harvests and fair weather.

We don't know what the Dagenham Idol represents – perhaps it's a god, or perhaps it's an offering to the gods. Because of the proximity of the deer skeleton – not butchered, but buried intact – it suggests that the idol was intentionally deposited, rather than lost or thrown away. The idol and the deer were laid together, but we don't know why. The fact that it was deposited at a time of change, when new people were arriving from the continent with tools and weapons made from a magical new material, metal, may be significant. Certainly, the people of Britain start to do things differently after this new culture arrives. But we don't know how numerous the incomers were, how speedy their arrival, or whether they caused trouble with the locals or were welcomed.

The wooden idol has survived for more than 4,000 years because of the marshy conditions – the thick peaty gloop of the riverside stopped oxygen reaching the wood, so bacteria couldn't rot it away. It may not have been an accident that people chose to put their idol in this type of waterlogged land: areas where land and water meet are liminal (neither one thing nor the other, on the threshold of both). Maybe this is where the spirits were closest, or where special rituals had to be performed.

Some archaeologists think the missing eye indicates that this is a supremely early representation of a god that eventually becomes Woden or Odin – the Anglo-Saxon and Norse god who sacrifices an eye in exchange for greater wisdom – for another example, see Sutton Hoo (page 85).

The hole at the crotch could be read two ways – as a symbol of womanhood and life-giving childbirth, or the place where there used to be a wooden phallus that's since been lost. The similarly shaped Broddenbjerg Idol from Denmark, also found in a peat bog, has an impressive foot-long phallus. It's just one of the many secrets the Dagenham Idol keeps.

Right The right eye socket is a deep, carved hole, the left is a small, chiselled dish shape. Is this a very ancient one-eyed god?

Lullingstone Roman Villa

Cryptic Christian messages hidden in the floor

Kent

Lullingstone possibly began life as the country retreat of the Roman governor of Britain. The preserved walls, artefacts and mosaics from generations of rich Roman homeowners are remarkable. So are the mysterious religious messages they conceal.

The mosaic in the reception room shows the mythical prince Bellerophon mounted on Pegasus, the winged horse, slaying the Chimera, a fire-breathing monster. Below that, princess Europa rides a bull, who's actually the god Jupiter in disguise. So far, so classical. But the inscription, a sophisticated couplet that riffs on the poetry of Virgil and Ovid, offers offers an elaborate wordsearch for Britain's earliest Christians:

> INVIDA SI TAURI VIDISSET IUNO NATATUS
> IUSTIUS AEOLIAS ISSET AD USQUE DOMOS

'INVIDA' is a word to ward off the evil eye. The rest reads: 'If jealous Juno [Jupiter's wife] had seen the swimming of the bull, more justly would she have gone to the palace of Aeolus [the west wind].')

Count eights from the end of INVIDA and you spell the name of the villa's owner, Avitus, and the word 'Vos' (You) (INVID**A** SI TAURI **V**IDISSET **I**UNO NATA**T**US IUSTI**U**S AEOLIA**S** ISSET AD **U**SQUE DOM**O**S INVIDA **S**I). Both lines start and end with 'I' and 'S', the first and last letters of Iesus (Jesus). Count eights in the second line and you spell the whole name, Jesus (**I**USTIUS A**E**OLIAS IS**S**ET AD USQ**U**E DOMO**S**). The word for God, DEUS, might also be hidden in there. Read together with the image, it suggests that for Avitus, Jesus offers salvation (if you choose to go with him, like Europa did by climbing on to Jupiter the bull); you, the non-believer, will be destroyed like a ship in a storm (as Juno demands Aeoleus the west wind should drown the Trojans, in the story of the Aeneid).

Initially this cryptic interpretation might seem fanciful, but well-educated Roman citizens loved these visual, literary puzzles. To design and commission this mosaic would have been a clever way to demonstrate your intellect, and a subtle way to demonstrate your Christian faith.

Christians were viciously persecuted until Roman Emperor Constantine's conversion in AD 313. The mosaic probably dates from the mid-300s, but these were early days and Avitus may have felt it remained dangerous to explicitly declare himself as Christian. By the 360s, however, times changed enough that the family built a Christian chapel within their home – it's the earliest surviving chapel we have in Britain. But mysteriously, it was built on top of an underground pagan shrine, which seems to have continued to be used. Was this someone hedging their bets, or trying to keep the whole family happy? Lullingstone reminds us that Romans weren't just militaristic road-builders, they were as spiritually complicated as the rest of us.

Left This remarkable mosaic has survived for 1,700 years. At the top, Bellerophon, mounted on Pegasus, slays the Chimera. In the middle is a panel of squares, hearts and swastikas. At the bottom, Europa rides on Jupiter disguised as a bull.

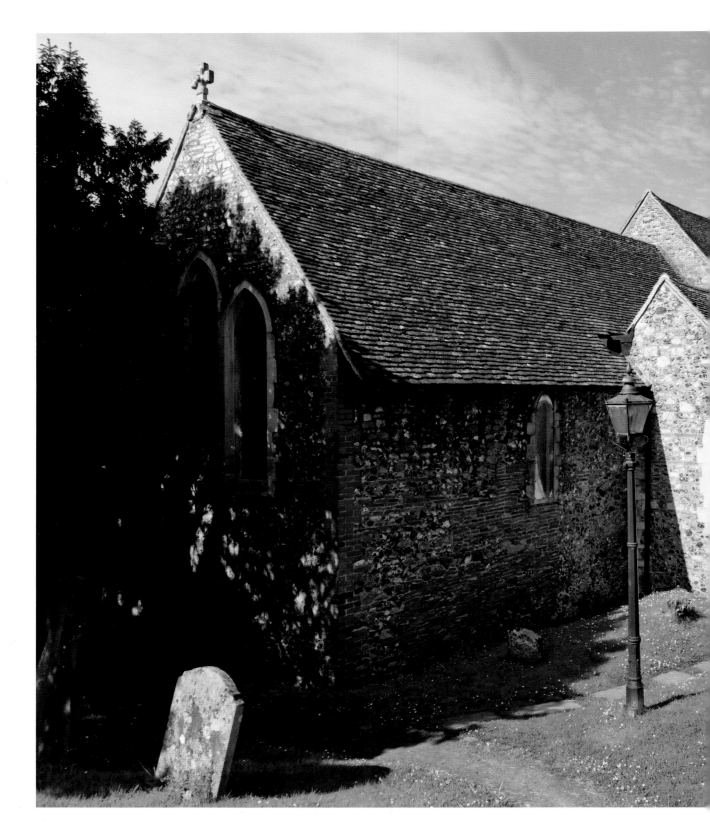

St Martin's Church

Britain's most ancient living church

Kent

Left Some time around AD 580 a Frankish princess named Bertha came to Canterbury to marry a prince of the pagan kingdom of Kent, Aethelbert.

Bertha's marriage was agreed on condition that she be allowed to continue to practise her Christian faith. She brought a bishop with her, and Aethelbert provided a building for her to use as a chapel. It was an old Roman structure, possibly originally a temple or mausoleum, solidly constructed from stone and brick. The original walls of the Roman building form the chancel walls of this church. When St Augustine arrived in Canterbury in AD 597, he based himself at Bertha's church. He baptised King Aethelbert, and as news spread, Bertha's church became too small for the gathering crowds. So the nave, the main body of the church, was rebuilt. It still stands much as it did then, constructed from reused Roman stone and brick, visible here in the walls. Christians have prayed in this church every day for more than 1,400 years.

Ringlemere Gold Cup

A ritual vessel from a lost monument

Kent

Above This delicate pure gold cup was made between the years 1700–1500 BC, during the Bronze Age. The body is beaten from a single sheet of gold, and the handle is attached with tiny gold rivets. It was found by a metal detectorist after it had been hit by a farmer's plough (hence the crumpled look). It may have originally been buried in someone's grave.

Its base is conical, so it was designed not to be put down – perhaps passed from hand to hand, or held by one important person. One other gold cup like this was discovered in Cornwall. Four others have been found in France, Germany and Switzerland, and there are similar cups made from shale, amber and silver. They're all in coastal regions, and it suggests that the prehistoric people of Ringlemere were linked to other seafaring peoples in sophisticated trading and cultural networks: an original European union.

Above This 2,000-year-old tankard can hold almost four pints. It's made of yew wood staves, with a metal handle and two bronze outer bands that would have shone a burnished golden colour when new. It dates to the late Iron Age or early Roman period, when native British culture appears to have been heavily focused on men's drinking rituals. Held in two hands by each drinker and passed around a group, this tankard would be used to share booze: a way for important people to show their generosity, affirm relationships and foster allegiances.

It was found in boggy ground, and nearby two decorated bronze bowls and a strainer for decanting wine or herbal infusions were also deposited. It suggests this watery edgeland was significant for ritual deposits. Perhaps these were gifts to the gods by local leaders of the Silures Welsh tribe, facing the advancing Roman army.

St Leonard's Ossuary

*Contemplating death,
the medieval way*

Kent

Right The underground crypt below St Leonard's parish church in Hythe, Kent, is home to 1,200 skulls and a vast stack of human bones 7 m (23 ft) long and 2 m (6 ft 6 in) high. That's around 2,000 men, women and children, who died from the 1200s to the 1500s, and were once buried in the consecrated ground of the churchyard. As the church was extended and the churchyard filled, their graves were unearthed and the surviving bones transferred to the ossuary. This was still sanctified ground, and prayers would be said to help the souls of the departed reach Heaven. Ossuaries became places of pilgrimage, where people would come to contemplate their mortality, pray for the souls of loved ones, and perhaps gawk at the extraordinary sight of so many bones. This meant they were targeted by the zealots of the Protestant Reformation in the mid-1500s, who believed bone houses to be superstitious and irreligious. Somehow the bones at St Leonard's survived (along with just one other in England, at Holy Trinity in Rothwell, Northamptonshire). They remain peculiar sites of pilgrimage to this day.

Knowlton Circles

The church inside an ancient henge

Dorset

Left Knowlton's Norman church sits within a prehistoric henge. At the top left of the picture, you can see the Great Barrow, covered in trees. Bottom right, another circular feature is visible as a crop mark. This ritual site has been important for more than 4,500 years.

Around the world there are traditions of holy rivers and sacred places, and it's possible that Knowlton Circles are the Dorset equivalent of a great temple by the River Ganges. There are five earthen circles, positioned in a natural landscape rich with mystical potential. On one side there's the confluence of the two tributaries of the River Allen. On the other side there's a field of natural sink holes – shafts that open up suddenly when the limestone below collapses. So this strange place sits between water and the underworld.

People began building earthworks in Knowlton around 2500 BC and used them for about a thousand years. Many of them are impressive, but one really stands out. In the centre of this Neolithic (late Stone Age) earthen ring, there's a medieval church. It perfectly demonstrates the idea that some places persist in importance, even when everything else – economy, technology, religion and race – changes.

The Knowlton site is complex, with five key elements. There's the circle with the church in it. The Southern Circle is the largest, at 230 m (755 ft) across. It has a farm in it. The Northern Circle has an odd causeway entrance and a strangely rectangular ditch inside it. The 'Old Churchyard' earthwork is odd too, and there's no evidence that it was ever used as a churchyard or cemetery, so the name is a mystery as well. And there's a massive burial mound, The Great Barrow, which has two rings of ditches round it. We don't know if the ditches came before the barrow, and it was an enclosure like the others, or perhaps the ditches and barrow were all constructed at the same time. Archaeologists have struggled to get reliable samples to date the site, so many questions remain.

We also don't know whether the circles were built and used at the same time, or what they were for. Hundreds of years after the first monuments were built here, the site became a focal point for burials, with a staggering 178 Bronze Age round barrows constructed within a mile. But before that, was it a place of life rituals or death rituals? It very probably witnessed both.

The church was built in the twelfth century, making it about the same date as Kilpeck church (page 181); the tower was added in the 1400s. It served as the parish church for a small village that was near the river, but when the village declined and everyone moved away, the church fell into ruin.

We don't know why the local people decided to site their church inside this ancient earthwork in the 1100s (church communities elsewhere destroyed their local prehistoric monuments because they didn't like the pagan wickedness). The earthworks would have been much clearer 900 years ago, and ripe with myth and legend. Knowlton is still said to be haunted, a place where magic is close. Perhaps that's a folk memory some 4,500 years in the making.

Stonehenge

Temple of the winter sun

Wiltshire

Left The monument we see today is the final phase of a site actively built and rebuilt for more than 1,500 years, from about 3000–1500 BC. The largest trios of stone form an inner horseshoe, and smaller freestanding bluestones form a circuit within an outer ring of sarsens. The unique Altar Stone is hidden under a fallen sarsen.

Nowadays, many people head to Stonehenge at Midsummer to celebrate the dawn on the longest day. The sun lights the inside of the circle, illuminating the highest stones on the western side. But if they want to celebrate the most important day, they're six months out. The most powerful alignment at Stonehenge is actually in the opposite direction – designed to mark the setting sun on Midwinter evening, the start of the longest night. On Midwinter's Eve, processing into the inner sanctum, facing the tallest, most impressive stones, you face south-west. The sun aligns perfectly to pierce rays into the heart of the monument, a burst of gold before darkness descends. For people in prehistoric Britain, Midwinter would have likely been a powerful moment in the calendar. Perhaps it was a symbolic time associated with realms of the spirits, or the dead. It may also have represented the eternal and essential cycle of regeneration, and the returning life force of spring.

Even though we don't fully understand it, this site, above all others, occupies a huge place in our collective psyche. It's why more than one and a half million people visit every year. Perhaps it's also why, when people first see Stonehenge, they're often struck by how small it is, compared to what they imagined. The stone circle at the heart of the monument is just 30 m (100 ft) across. But within this compact circle, there is staggering complexity and scale: the largest sarsen stones, stacked like Jenga blocks, are on average 25 tonnes each – about the weight of four fully grown African bull elephants. And the whole thing sits within a ceremonial landscape of global archaeological importance, that was actively shaped and remodelled for more than 1,500 years, from about 3000–1500 BC.

Every element of this remarkable monument is strange. The first thing the builders constructed was an earthwork circle with an outer bank, ditch and inner bank. Then they dug a ring of fifty-six holes inside the inner bank and erected either timber posts or standing stones in them.

Above Protruding tenon on the Great Trilithon. This would have fit into the matching 'mortise' hole in the lintel stone, a technique more common to woodworking than stonemasonry.

But before the stones went into these holes, now known as the Aubrey holes, they were used to deposit human cremations. Cremated remains have also been found in the bottom of the encircling ditch, and at other spots within the henge. It's difficult to be certain how many individuals are represented in the burned bone fragments, but at the very least we have the remains of 150 men, women and children. Incredibly, this makes Stonehenge the largest known Neolithic cemetery, and that's just from the areas that have been excavated. About half of the Aubrey holes remain unexcavated, so further truths have yet to be unearthed. Chemical analysis of the excavated bones show that some of the individuals grew up in west Wales, and others travelled regularly between the Stonehenge area and west Wales. These communities were more than 200 km (125 miles) apart but for some mysterious reason they were linked. We don't know whether everybody had the right to burial at Stonehenge, or whether it was only for the select few. We also don't know if the site was only used for death rites, or other ceremonies as well.

The next phase of building is the one that transforms Stonehenge from remarkable to incredible. Around 2500 BC, some 500 years after the henge was begun, the people erected a circle of sarsen stones inside the earthwork, four 'station stones' at the edges of the circle and an inner horseshoe of five huge trilithons. The name is from tri- ('three'), -lith ('stone'): trios of stones with two uprights and a lintel on top. They also arranged bluestones into arcs. The people shaped the sarsen stones carefully, and chipped off all the weathered stone so that they would gleam white. Recent laser-scanning analysis of the trilithons has shown that the inner faces and north-east sides – the sides that face the entrance – were more carefully finished than the others.

The sarsen stones are a local sandstone, probably brought from about 30 km (19 miles) away on the Marlborough Downs. 'Sarsen' is a corruption of 'Saracen stone', a medieval term originally used to describe Arab Muslims, but repurposed to describe anything mysteriously non-Christian. The largest trio of sarsens in the central horseshoe is known as the Great Trilithon. Originally it would have stood about 9 m (30 ft) high, with around 2 m (6 ft 7 in) of stone sunk into the ground. Unfortunately, only one of the great uprights is now standing, the other remains where it fell. On the top of the standing upright you can see a protruding knob – this would have fitted into a circular hole in the underside of the lintel. These joints are known as 'mortise and tenon', a method more commonly used in woodwork. To achieve the level of accuracy required to make mortise and tenon joints on such massive stones, and then manoeuvre them into place, is a feat of engineering and construction brilliance.

Frustratingly, when the Great Trilithon fell, it squashed one of the most mysterious elements of the monument, the so-called Altar Stone. The impact of the falling trilithon was so great that it actually semi-buried the Altar Stone, which means that it's never been fully analysed. What we do know is that it's a totally different kind of stone from the rest of Stonehenge, a type of old sandstone quarried from South Wales. It could have started off as a standing stone, but it's more likely that it was laid flat, and perhaps used as a platform or altar. Maybe offerings were made here, or it served as a frame upon which the Midwinter sun could set on to (a bit like the recumbent stone circles of Aberdeenshire, page 35).

The bluestones are perhaps the best-known part of the Stonehenge mystery. They were quarried from outcrops in the Preseli hills in west Wales some 200 km (125 miles) away (page 185) – from the same area as some of the people whose cremated remains were buried at Stonehenge in the earliest phases. They weigh 2–5 tonnes each, and the achievement of getting them here – either by land, sea or river – is astonishing. A number of them have tongue-and-groove joints along their lengths so they could be slotted tightly together, while others have circular mortise holes so they might work as lintels, sitting on top of other stones. We don't have any evidence that the stones were ever positioned in this way at Stonehenge, so it suggests that they started life in other monuments – in an unknown location – before being dispatched for use here.

The bluestones have moved a lot. There's evidence that they were the original stones set into the Aubrey holes, which would mean that they were here at the beginning of everything, around 3000 BC. Then around 2500 BC they were arranged into a double arc inside the sarsen circle. They were rearranged again around 300 years later, around 2200 BC, to form a circle and a horseshoe, which is how we see the monument today. We don't know whether this later remodelling was the work of new people arriving in the area, or local people modifying the monument to fit changing times. It's sometimes quite tricky to puzzle out the arrangements when you look at the modern monument, as many of the sarsens and bluestones are fallen or missing. This place has been famous for a long time, and it's very likely that some of the missing stones were carted off as souvenirs, as well as being used for more prosaic jobs like filling potholes in local roads. Intriguingly, it appears that some of the bluestones were intentionally broken off to just leave stumps long before the modern era – was this an episode of ritualised destruction by prehistoric people?

The mystery continues with the Avenue. It's an earthwork corridor leading 2.8 km (1¾ miles) from the banks of the River Avon to the entrance to the henge, and was constructed around 2300 BC. It originally had high banks and 2-m (6 ft 7 in-) deep ditches on either side of the path. It's designed like a processional route, but the Avenue isn't compacted or hollowed in the way you'd expect of a heavily used pathway, so it can't have been open to many visitors. And of course Stonehenge had been in use for centuries before the Avenue was even constructed. So why did later people suddenly build an avenue, which they then didn't use very much?

Below Many of the Aubrey holes (marked as red dots inside the green earthwork circle) haven't been excavated, but are likely to contain human cremations – they may hold the key to understanding the people who began Stonehenge.

The first Stonehenge c.3000 BC

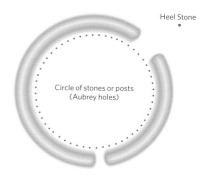

Heel Stone

Circle of stones or posts (Aubrey holes)

The stones arrive c.2500 BC

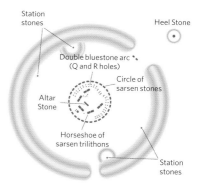

Station stones

Heel Stone

Double bluestone arc (Q and R holes)

Circle of sarsen stones

Altar Stone

Horseshoe of sarsen trilithons

Station stones

The bluestones rearranged c.2200 BC

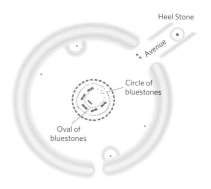

Heel Stone

Avenue

Circle of bluestones

Oval of bluestones

At the time the bluestones were rearranged and the Avenue built, hundreds of circular burial mounds were constructed in the surrounding landscape. It looks like religion and ritual practices changed as the Stone Age transitioned into the Bronze Age, but Stonehenge continued to be spiritually relevant. Perhaps the Avenue was only used during these later burial ceremonies, where the most-favoured individuals would be transported along the river to Stonehenge and paraded to the stones, before being taken on to the site of their burial mound and last resting place. More circuits of holes were dug around the stones some time between 1800–1500 BC but they were left mysteriously unfilled. The builders might have planned to rearrange Stonehenge's stones once more, but it never happened. What they did do, however, was carve graffiti of bronze axeheads and daggers on to the surfaces of the sarsens. Perhaps this was a way to maintain the ancient site's relevance to Bronze Age people, or for new migrants (perhaps metal workers from the continent) to claim it as their own.

Who built Stonehenge? Three kilometres (1⅞ miles) north-east of the circle is the site of Durrington Walls. Archaeologists have discovered that,

for about a decade, this site was probably the home of the construction workforce of Stonehenge, around 2500 BC. Hundreds of hut circles with hard earth floors and wooden frames were built. There was a large circular monument made of concentric rings of wooden posts constructed near the centre of the village, facing towards Midwinter sunrise. We don't know whether the people who built Stonehenge were slaves or servants, or whether they worked gladly and voluntarily, perhaps as a devotional act. What we do know from Durrington Walls is that at least some of them were eating very well. Over 38,000 discarded animal bones were found, from at least 1,000 animals, mostly pigs and cattle. Isotope analysis of the animals' teeth showed that many of them came from west Wales (the original home of the bluestones and those cremated human remains), but also from northern England and Scotland. They must have been driven here 'on the hoof' or shipped in by boat before being slaughtered and cooked. Were these animals herded by people attending events at Stonehenge? Or were they traded to people who were accumulating as many animals as they could afford? Maybe the Welsh pigs followed the same route as the bluestones? Many of the pigs were around nine months old when they were slaughtered, which suggests a spring birth and slaughter in December. They also had abnormally decayed teeth, which suggests they were being fed a sweet diet, perhaps to make their flesh tastier. When the joints and carcasses of the animals were thrown into rubbish dumps, they still had a lot of meat on the bones – so clearly this wasn't just cooking to assuage hunger, this was cooking for show.

The people living in the Stone Age were mostly subsistence farmers, and it's hard for us to envisage how they would have ever had the time and resources to construct Stonehenge. To imagine they were also throwing away food turns most of our preconceptions on their heads. But Stonehenge and Durrington Walls were not everyday places. There's surely a link between the design of Stonehenge to mark Midwinter and the winter meat feasts at Durrington. We don't know what these festivities were, or how they were related to activity at Stonehenge, but they were definitely displays of excess at the darkest time of year. It's a tradition that continues to this day, with laden tables and indigestion at Christmas, along with marking the cycle of the seasons (evergreen wreaths and Christmas trees), celebrating light (baubles, candles, fires and fairy lights) and gathering as families and communities to sing songs, perform pantomimes and kiss under the mistletoe. Perhaps our Stone Age ancestors are not so distant after all.

Bush Barrow Dagger

A chief's treasures

Wiltshire

Right This chief was buried near Stonehenge around 1950 BC, when the area was still very important. He was buried with a large gold lozenge, a gold belt buckle and numerous weapons. The outstanding piece, however, is the handle of his dagger (inset): it's decorated in a zigzag pattern with 140,000 individually made gold studs. Each is thinner than a human hair, less than 1 mm ($\frac{1}{32}$ in) in length, and set into the handle to overlap like glimmering fish scales. It's likely children were used for this work, and that more than one of them would have lost their eyesight to create this masterpiece.

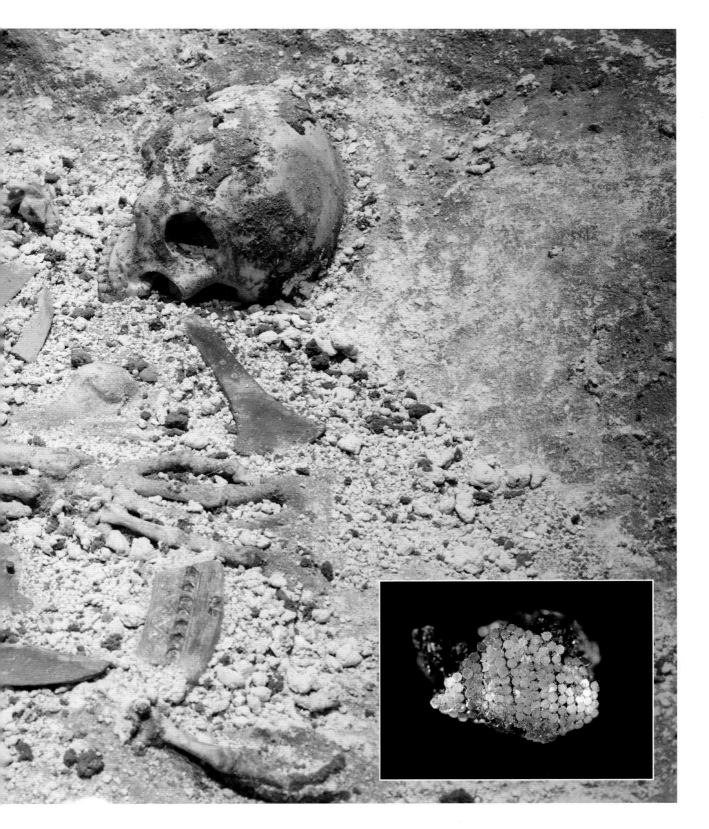

Avebury

*The world's largest
stone circle*

Wiltshire

Left This Neolithic ceremonial complex is so large it dwarfs the modern village. Avebury was built around 2850 BC, and continued to be modified for more than 600 years. The Great Henge is vast – almost 500 m (1,640 ft) in diameter – and originally the bank towered 17 m (56 ft) above a 9 m (30 ft) deep ditch. Within the 'superhenge' there's a huge circle which was originally formed of around 100 colossal stones, with two smaller stone circles inside that, which in turn enclosed additional complicated stone and wooden stake arrangements. Avebury was a place for performing ritual, concealing ritual, processions and demonstrations of authority – perhaps both sacred and political. It continues to enthral, almost 5,000 years later.

Silbury Hill

The biggest mound in Europe

Wiltshire

Left This entirely artificial hill is some 4,400 years old. It took about 4 million hours of labour to construct.

This is the largest man-made mound in Europe. It's around 4,400 years old, about the same age as the Great Pyramid of Giza in Ancient Egypt. It contains half a million tonnes of chalk and soil, dug by hand with wooden shovels and pickaxes made from deer antlers. It's estimated that it took at least 4 million hours of labour to construct. But what we see today isn't the result of one frenzied building spree – this strange hill is the work of three generations of people who returned to this spot time and time again.

Excavations completed in 2007 revealed that Silbury has a dizzying series of building phases. The first mound was just a 1-m (3 ft 3 in-) pile of gravel, probably gathered from the nearby River Kennet. Years later, people heaped soil over the gravel. They dug and refilled small groups of pits and ditches multiple times. And then they built the big one – the thirteen-storey hill we see today. It took at least eighty years for the mound to reach its peak – 31 m (102 ft) high and 160 m (525 ft) in diameter.

The A4 road running alongside Silbury has origins that go back at least as far as the Romans. It seems raised, but that's actually the original level of the land surface. The ground surrounding the hill was dug out during the final stages of construction to form a large ditch. On the western side the builders extended the ditch into a wide rectangle. This area regularly floods, and then this mystical mound appears to float in its own shimmering pool. Maybe this watery effect was why they built it. The fact that the mound is almost sunk into the surrounding land suggests that perhaps the mystical importance of this mound is not about its height and prominence, but about the water beneath and around it.

Silbury is situated at the confluence of a number of springs and seasonal streams known as 'winterbournes'. These form the River

Below Flooding in 2019 reveals
how much the ground around
the hill was dug out during
construction, enabling it to
transform into an almost-island.
Water is an integral part of
Silbury's purpose.
Right The Swallowhead Springs,
near Silbury Hill. These feed the
River Kennet and ultimately the
Thames. The colourful ribbons
in the trees are offerings from
modern water-worshippers.

Kennet and ultimately feed into the River Thames. In cultures across the world, the heads of important rivers are revered. The point where water first flows from the earth is often sacred and protected. Silbury Hill rises with the rising water. Maybe this enormous hill marks a sacred place. There's another huge mound in Marlborough, also along the River Kennet, and we know that in the Vale of Pewsey nearby there was a mound (now destroyed) known as Hatfield Barrow, that sits alongside the River Avon. Maybe the people who built these mounds were claiming the water, and the sacred power that came with it.

What's certain is that these hills were constructed at a time when life was changing rapidly in this part of prehistoric Britain – communities were starting to bury people in individual graves rather than communal tombs. New types of pottery and the first metal artefacts were introduced, marking the end of the Stone Age and the start of the Bronze Age. The archaeological evidence is tentative, but it appears that new people were bringing these new tools and skills. Silbury could have been a vast earthen gesture to show the newcomers who this land really belonged to.

Around the hill, you'll still find small offerings from people drawn to this enigmatic mound, almost five millennia later.

Childrey Warren

Death and deviant burial in the Iron Age

Oxfordshire

It's a picturesque and sleepy corner of Oxfordshire, but the villages of Letcombe Bassett and Letcombe Regis have been hiding a few dark secrets. In the fields nearby, archaeologists discovered a settlement area, Childrey Warren, where people were living from the Iron Age and into the Roman period, perhaps for as long as 800 BC through to AD 400. The archaeologists found evidence of houses, outbuildings and plots for yards and gardens. There were household items – pieces of broken pottery, knife blades and a particularly attractive decorated bone comb. And there were also more than thirty human bodies.

In the Roman period most people were buried in cemeteries at settlement boundaries or along roads. But the Iron Age had a diverse and complex range of mortuary activities. Some regions preferred cremation, others burial, and practices changed a lot over time. Overall, though, we don't have enough bodies to tally with the number of people who must have been alive. It seems like most dead bodies were disposed of in a way that hasn't left traces for twenty-first-century archaeologists. Perhaps they were cremated but their ashes weren't collected or buried, or their bodies were exposed in a form of sky burial, and the remains scattered in the wind.

Sometimes the Iron Age bodies we do find are in pretty strange places; the most common is at the bottom of a pit. These haven't been dug as graves; rather, they're usually circular storage pits in the heart of a village, reused to bury men, women or children. Pit burials are common enough that we can be sure they're a collective cultural activity, rather than the work of a prehistoric serial killer (or a very odd village council). Not everybody got buried in a pit though, and most pits didn't get used for burials. So why some people and some pits got this treatment, we don't know.

The excavations at Childrey Warren uncovered forty Iron Age

Above Some of the later burials at Childrey Warren are also classed as 'deviant'. This Roman Briton was decapitated after death and his head placed by his feet.

pits, and three of them held human remains. One contained the body of a newborn baby. Another held a child and part of a cow. The third, Pit 1863, was the most astonishing. A young woman, aged between twenty-five and twenty-nine, was placed on her back with her legs wide open, bent at the knee. Her arms were draped up and over her head. Her feet had been chopped off at the ankles and carefully placed next to her chest. Unfortunately the edges of the leg bones were damaged in the soil, so we don't have any evidence to indicate what kind of tool or weapon was used to remove the feet. Her arms are surprising too. Most people buried in pits have their arms by their sides, or in their laps. Her hands are gathered by her head – were her hands tied? Or were her arms arranged in this tableau on purpose?

The woman's body creates a dramatic visual display, but it wouldn't have been seen for long. After her legs were arranged, the pit must have been quickly filled with soil, otherwise they would have flopped further open rather than be held in position.

Below the body, in the same pit but buried earlier, was the corpse of a small dog. Below the dog, at the very bottom of the pit, were the delicate bones of a one- or two-year-old child. We don't yet know whether the woman and the baby are related, or how they're linked to the other children in the other pits. The researchers hope that radiocarbon dating and DNA testing will shed more light on the connections.

Some people have suggested that the position – and possible link to the baby – indicate that the woman died in childbirth. It's possible, but lying on your back to give birth is a relatively modern phenomenon. On a more global scale, women are more likely to labour kneeling or crouching, unless instructed otherwise. Even if the woman had died in childbirth, it still doesn't explain how she ended up in the pit like that – someone would have had to move her and then rearrange her body back into this strange position. Besides, death during childbirth would have been relatively common, so why was this woman picked out for special treatment?

Alternatively, this spread-eagled position could suggest something sexual, or a more abstract, symbolic representation of fertility. Was this a posthumous insult, or profoundly powerful, even magical? We just don't know.

The final suggestion is that this burial and positioning is actually part of a local tradition – other bodies in Iron Age Oxfordshire have been found buried in pits sitting up with their legs crossed. Maybe our spread-eagled lady is a form of cross-legged burial, it's just they took her feet off first. Could the villagers have worried that she might return from the grave and cause trouble in the living world? Maybe taking her feet off would stop her corpse from wandering, but leaving them neatly in the grave would mean she'd have them in the afterlife.

Further dating analysis will tell us more about the order the pit burials were made, how much time stands between each one and whether they're contemporary with the nearest houses.

What is clear is that the Childrey lady was intentionally buried in the heart of the community. It may have been so the living could keep an eye on her, or so she could keep an eye on the living. Theories abound – was she a criminal being punished or a human sacrifice, intentionally killed to appease the gods, or to seek blessings for bountiful harvests, success in warfare or safe deliverance from contagion? Maybe she wasn't killed intentionally, but the way she died meant her body had to be dealt with in a special way. Pit 1863 tells a story. Whether it's a story of the lucky and sacred, or the shamed and dangerous, we don't yet know.

Below Britain is full of archaeological sites like this – discovered by accident and bursting with incredible evidence of the strange lives of our ancestors.

Uffington White Horse

Bronze Age sun and horse worship

Oxfordshire

Left An unbroken chain of people have maintained this ancient hill figure, or 'geoglyph' for 3,000 years. It's a horse, but it does have a funny shaped head. And a beak.

This is the oldest hill figure in the country, and it's a beauty. Close up, it's hard to see how the lines fit together, but stand a few hundred metres away and you'll see an elongated equine body, lean and light, flowing across the undulations of the hillside. The horse gallops above an unusual natural feature called the Manger, a dry valley with springs at its base, and a low round knoll, Dragon Hill, to one side. Another 200 m (655 ft) further up the hill is a large hillfort enclosure known as Uffington Castle.

Archaeologists have dated the horse by taking samples from the soil directly below the lowest level of chalk and testing them with a technique called 'optically stimulated luminescence dating'. It determines when quartz particles in the soil were last exposed to sunlight. The sun last shone down on the soil under the horse at the end of the Bronze Age, or start of the Iron Age, between 1200–800 BC. It means the horse is about 3,000 years old.

The fact that it has survived means that an unbroken chain of 150 generations of people have climbed the hill to preserve it, pulling out the encroaching grass and repacking the outline with fresh chalk, pounded into place. If just one generation of people had decided not to bother, the horse would have disappeared into the hillside, and been lost forever. But if you look closely at the ground around the chalk lines, you'll see raised sections that extend beyond the white – some parts of the horse were originally wider, or longer, than they are now.

There are elements that puzzle – the ears aren't very 'horsey' and it has two distinctly odd whiskers on its chin (sometimes described as a beak). And even though it's one of the most remarkable pieces of land art in the world, it's not been built in the best place to make it visible; it sits across the flattened shoulder of the hill, rather than on the steepest slope. This means you can't see it from far away, and even with a good view, it takes a while for the eye to translate the abstract forms into 'horse'.

It probably means the horse wasn't primarily intended to be a territorial marker declaring that you were in the land of the White Horse people. So is the figure a picture for the gods, or is it a picture of a god?

In Sweden and Denmark, rock carvings and portable artworks of similar stylised horses have been dated to the same time as the Uffington figure. In fact, at this time, across a wide swathe of Europe and Asia, the horse is consistently associated with the sky and sun. So much so, that the 'Sun Horse' is believed to be a universal symbol of a lost world religion. Each day, the Sun Horse takes the sun through the sky, either pulling it directly or by drawing it on a chariot. The sun then journeys through the underworld, often on a boat, and at dawn

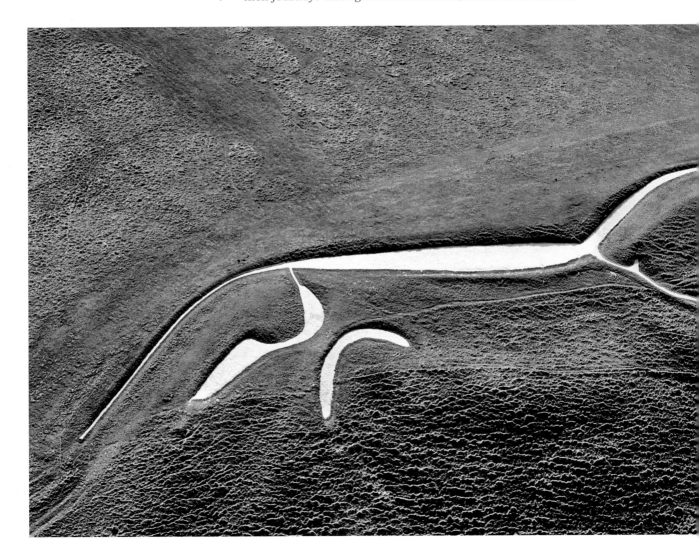

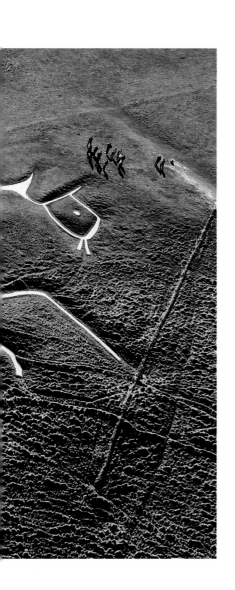

rises once more. Without the horse, there would be no sun. Without the sun, there would be no life. Horses, then, drew together light and dark, day and night, land and water in the eternal, essential cycle of life. Forensic analysis of Indo-European languages suggest that beliefs about the sun and the horse spread from Iran and India at the same time as the spread of the actual domestic horse.

The Uffington figure performs a piece of landscape theatre. This Sun Horse is perhaps on the shoulder of the hill because that's what puts it closest to the sky. Around Midwinter, the sun is so low it almost rolls across the horse's back. Rising in the east, the sun casts its light across the hill on to the horse's head. As the day progresses, sunlight tracks across its body until dusk, when light falls upon the tail. In the dark, we know the horse will pull the sun beyond sight, to return tomorrow.

Some archaeologists have also associated Wayland's Smithy, the late Stone Age tomb nearby, with the Sun Horse. This chambered tomb was already a thousand years old when the horse was constructed, but the Bronze Age people may have reconjured it as a portal, perhaps where the horse and sun could enter the underworld.

But – and this is the difficulty – if everyone in Europe believed in the power of the Sun Horse, why is Europe not covered with Sun Horses, as the Christian world is with crosses? We do see stylised horses very like Uffington on the Iron Age coins made by the people in Oxfordshire, the Atrebates tribe, usually depicted with the crescent moon and a wheel shape that may represent the sun, or a chariot. But these are later – minted from 300 BC onwards. Even if you allow for some horses to have disappeared in the intervening three millennia, we would still expect more than we have. The best suggestion is that Uffington was, for some reason, special.

One intriguing theory is that the horse sprang into life as the result of a landslip. Overnight perhaps, some sections of turf loosened from the chalk bedrock below and slumped downhill. The lines of exposed white chalk happened to look vaguely horse-like, and that was enough to inspire the locals; a miraculous image of the Sun Horse had revealed itself! The landslip was then augmented to become ever more equine. Whether the work was done by slaves or willing devotees, we don't know.

The horse certainly has devotees now. Every year people from around the world come to this hillside to do their bit to keep the horse alive, investing time and energy in heritage, community and tradition. And quite possibly enacting a ritual that began with the origins of the domestic horse in Britain, some 3,000 years ago.

Headington Mandrake

Malevolent roots with a deep history

Oxfordshire

Legend has it that the mandrake only grows under a gallows, and takes its humanlike form because of the bodily substances that drop to the ground at the execution site. When you pull up a mandrake, it screams. And hearing the scream can kill you.

The earliest mentions of the mandrake's magical properties are by the Roman historian Josephus, writing in the first century AD. He describes using a dog to dig them up, so the dog dies from the screaming, rather than you. The association with the gallows comes later – from the German Otto Brunfels, who quotes the Persian writer Avicenna, and says that mandrakes grow from the spilled semen of men dying on the gallows.

John Gerard's *Herball*, a botany book first published in 1597, has a chapter on mandrakes. Gerard begins by describing the plant as having 'great broad long smooth leaves of a darke greene colour', with fruits 'a yellowish colour, smooth, soft and glittering, of a strong smell'. Then he gets to the bit that makes the mandrake perhaps the most magical of all British plants. 'The root is long, thicke, whitish, divided many times into two or three parts resembling the legs of a man, with other parts of the body adjoyning thereto.' But he reassures his readers that he himself has dug up, planted and replanted plenty of mandrakes. There was no screaming, no death, no magic.

And yet this root was in the possession of an Oxfordshire farm labourer in 1916, some 300 years later. It's actually black briony, but he believed it was a mandrake and that it had magical properties, on account of its human form. It was collected by folklorists and eventually made its way into the collection of the famed Pitt Rivers Museum in Oxford.

The Headington Mandrake was used to promote fertility and good fortune – either by carrying it about or by hiding it in the house and caring for it like a talismanic dolly. Parts of it may also have been infused and the liquid either drunk as a herbal tea or sprinkled on windowsills, doorways and on livestock to protect or cure them from sickness.

With such demand for these mystical roots over the centuries, there was a healthy trade in fakes. Both white and black briony roots were often passed off as mandrake, and sharp dealers would judiciously prune the roots into ever more humanlike shapes. They were even known to dip turnips in fat and hair to create mandrake men they could sell to the unsuspecting.

John Gerard does say that that mandrake can be used to 'cool and dry' the humours, soothe pain in the eyes, purge excess phlegm and help mothers through the labour of a stillborn baby. He was writing at a time of great scientific development. Leading thinkers argued that observation of the natural world and the rational deduction of cause and consequence should take the place of superstition. Gerard urges us: plants are certainly medicinal, but they are not magical. But even now, for many of us, it's hard to look the Headington Mandrake in the eye and entirely agree.

Cirencester Mother Goddesses

A forgotten cult

Gloucestershire

Left This carving was discovered during excavations in Cirencester, on the site of a possible temple. The mothers wear cloaks and hold baskets containing loaves of bread, apples and an unidentifiable third food.

The Ancient Romans had a method for ruling their numerous territories – if a local custom didn't harm the Empire, they'd tolerate it. If there was a local god or goddess similar to one they already knew, then the two would intermingle – known as syncretism – to form one belief system. If there wasn't an obvious Roman deity to pair a local god with, you'd simply make offerings to the new god alongside your own gods – good sense, when you were in the wilds of a barbarian land at the mercy of local fates.

Sulis (a Celtic healing and life-giving goddess) and Minerva (the Roman goddess), for example, blend to become Sulis Minerva, goddess of wisdom and healing, and the primary deity at the temple at Bath (known as Aquae Sulis). But Sulis appears in other guises too. In Roman Gloucestershire, these three women came to be known as the Sulivae, linking them to the cult of Sulis. In Germany, they're worshipped as the Matrones, and in Gaul (modern France) as the Matres: these are the Mothers.

The Mothers are a trio, usually sitting, sometimes holding babies or small children, and sometimes holding food in baskets – one has apples (or other fruits), another loaves of bread. They're occasionally found singly, alongside the Genii Cucullati, the Hooded Spirits (page 39) or with animals or plants. Are they providers and protectors, nurturing and gentle? Or does the fruit they're holding represent a demand for offerings? Maybe they're vengeful, powerful figures – keep them happy and they'll be on your side; neglect them at your peril. The way we interpret the role of these mothers may say more about modern expectations of women, than it tells us about Romano-British cult worship.

'Triplism' is a common characteristic in pre-Roman Celtic religions, and triple goddesses appear in many ancient European faiths: the Norse Norns, who weave the fate of all living things; and the Irish Morrigan, who is both three and one great queen at once. We don't know if the Mothers were three distinct entities, or three aspects of one goddess, but 'threeness' seems central. One carving from Corinium – the Roman name for Cirencester – depicts just one Mother, but instead she's holding three apples.

Despite the fact that this was a literate society, we don't have any written descriptions of the cult of the Sulivae Mothers. It doesn't appear to be a secretive cult, so it may be that people just didn't see the point of writing something down that seemed so self-evident at the time. What's clear is that these women were particularly popular in Corinium, where temple sites appear full of evidence of the Mothers. Corinium started life as the tribal capital of the Iron Age Dobunni and flourished as a prosperous multicultural, commercial hub in Roman times. The Mothers also flourished for centuries. They probably began life as Celtic goddesses before the Romans arrived, but it's clear their fortunes fell when the Romans left. No one brought more apples, and the Mothers were forgotten.

Roman Baby's Cockerel

An underworld companion for a lost child

Gloucestershire

This enigmatic little object was buried and never meant to be seen again. It was found in the grave of a two-year-old child in Cirencester who died some time between AD 100–200. We don't know if the child was a boy or girl, what their name was or the cause of their death. But inside the wooden coffin, they were wearing hobnailed shoes, beads and bracelets and had a pottery feeding bottle that once contained milk.

It's a richly furnished grave and indicates the wealth of the child's family, as well as the care they wanted to show for their baby, even after death. Romans were not so different from modern parents; they worried for their kids. Talismans and charms would be tied on cradles and worn as bracelets to protect from the evil eye, and gods and spirits would be invoked to protect the child when it slept, ate and played. But if your child died, what more could you do?

The cockerel is exquisite. It's 12 cm (4¾ in) high, and stands with its tail fanned and its beak open as if crowing. It's made of moulded bronze, with inlaid enamelling on the comb, eyes, tail, breast and wings. The enamel now looks blue and green, but was originally bright shades of blue, yellow and red. There are only eight enamelled cockerels like this one known from across the whole Roman Empire, so it's a rare thing indeed. We don't know where it was made, but it could be from a workshop in Britain, possibly in Castleford, West Yorkshire, which was renowned for its enamelling work and exported its wares across the Roman world.

Cockerels were associated with the god Mercury, a messenger for the gods and shepherd for deceased souls on the journey to the afterlife. This was an arduous and potentially dangerous journey – and knowing your child would face it alone must have been agonising. So it's possible the cockerel in the grave was a gift for Mercury, to ask for his protection for the child on their journey to the underworld and their soul's final rest.

Another interpretation is that it's a toy, but it's unwieldy (constructed from separate parts that you need to hold together) and would have been phenomenally expensive. Other children's graves from the Roman period do contain figurines and dolls that appear to be toys – either specially bought for the funeral, or ones loved and played with in life. Although child mortality in Roman Britain was higher than it is in modern Britain, this little figure is just part of the evidence that shows children were often mourned as keenly as they are now. In these intimate histories, we're afforded a vivid picture of an individual in life. Perhaps our baby with the cockerel would have fit the epitaph found on another child's tomb in Rome: DUM VIXI, LUSI. 'All the time I lived, I played.'

The Rollright Witch

An Anglo-Saxon mystic princess

Warwickshire

Since the first antiquarian records of the Rollright Stones, there have been reports of a Rollright Witch, a woman of the stones, responsible for turning living men into monoliths. Tall tales aren't often confirmed by the archaeological record – but a skeleton and its mysterious grave goods recently unearthed from this site really do suggest someone linked to the supernatural.

The Rollright Stones themselves are actually a collection of monuments spread across two fields, spanning thousands of years of human ritual activity. There's the central circle, known as the King's Men. It originally formed a continuous wall with extra stones marking an entryway on the south-eastern side, and was built around 2500 BC, making it very early for a stone circle. Downhill, about 400 m (1,300 ft) away, you can see the remains of the Whispering Knights chambered tomb. It's incredibly old – perhaps from as early as 3800 BC. Over the road, there's a gnarled tooth of weathered limestone, the King Stone, which dates to 1500 BC and originally marked a cemetery of Bronze Age burials and cremations.

The 'witch' burial was found just metres from the King Stone, but it isn't Bronze Age. It dates to the mid-600s AD, making it more than a thousand years younger. Forensic analysis revealed that it was an Anglo-Saxon woman who was about twenty-five to thirty years old when she died, with no indication for cause of death on her skeleton. She was buried on her back, south to north, with her head to the south; one of her hands was laid in her lap, the other was positioned to grasp a rock that had been carefully buried with her.

The items in her grave show she was wealthy and are described by even the most conservative archaeologists as 'amuletic' – magical items. There was a circular deer antler disc behind her back, an animal's tooth beneath her head and a large amber bead, which

was probably attached to her clothes or hair. A round-headed pin was found near her nose, which may have been a shroud pin or for holding a headscarf in place. A silver and amethyst strip was found by her left arm and a large rock crystal bead, cut with eight facets, was by her waist, possibly suspended on an iron chain. This could be a special spindle whorl (page 63). Next to her head was a strange long-handled bronze pan, known as a patera or trulleum. The corroded remains of a lock and hinges indicate it had been placed in a lockable wooden box.

The trulleum is an artefact more commonly associated with the Byzantine Empire, centered in modern-day Turkey, rather than the Cotswolds. It would have been used in ritual hand washing, perhaps before ceremonies or feasts. Water would be poured from a special jug on to the hands, and the person holding this long-handled pan would catch the water below. It's not clear whether the lady in the grave would have been the one having her hands washed, or whether she was performing or directing the washing. In other circumstances, servants would perform these tasks, but if this were a high-status or secret ceremony or ritual, then maybe a special person would do it. And this woman was clearly special.

We don't know this woman's name, and we can only guess at her role in life. Was she a wife and mother? Or do all the mystical artefacts suggest that she was different, with special duties and special powers? She came to the Rollright Stones in death, but maybe this was a place she came to in life, too? Maybe the stories of a witch really do point towards a folk memory of a strange woman who lived among the stones, had command of the supernatural and was able to wield power over both ghosts and kings? But she died young, and we can only guess at the personal grief or political turmoil her early death may have caused.

There's a large Saxon cemetery near by that was in use at the time the woman died. But for whatever reason, her family decided that she would be buried at the Stones instead. We don't know if the woman was Christian. The transitional period when Christianity was first being introduced has people buried in all orientations, not just east–west, and they continue to use grave goods, unlike later Christian burials. But this was certainly a time of great political and religious change, and high-status women were educated and respected as queens, abbottesses and leaders. Nearby at West Hanney, archaeologists have found another high-status female burial and enigmatic artefacts like the Baldehildis Seal (page 74) show how 'Dark Age' women could be literate and independent rulers.

The people living here in the 600s wouldn't have known the historical details of the Neolithic and Bronze Age monuments at

Above The trulleum is a utensil used for ritual hand washing, more commonly associated with the Byzantine Empire in the eastern Mediterranean.

Rollright, but it was clearly a landscape that meant something to them. They may have used the circle for their own rituals, or regarded it as a sacred, or dangerous space. Rollright is now on the border of Oxfordshire and Warwickshire, and in the seventh century, it was on the border of the Hwicce kingdom. Maybe the young woman died at a time her family needed to emphasise their entitlement to this land, and the enduring nature of their authority. What better way than to bury a beloved young woman at the heart of the ancient site. Especially if she were a woman who was powerful and strange, in life and death.

Cerne Abbas Giant

A naked pagan Hercules?

Dorset

The Giant is immediately recognisable. Not only does he stand 60 m (200 ft) high, he is stark naked and has an enormous, erect penis. The other famous human-like hillfigure in Britain, the Long Man of Wilmington, is also naked but he doesn't boast any anatomical details to rival the Giant's.

A geophysical survey of the area and comparison with eighteenth-century illustrations, suggests that he may have originally had a belly button above his penis, but in Victorian times the chalk outline was modified to incorporate the two and make him particularly well-endowed. These days it would be a criminal offence, but there is something peculiarly (and delightfully) British about a bunch of people secretly drawing a big knob on a hillside.

Geophysics also indicates that the giant has lost something draped over his left arm. This suggests he's a representation of the Roman god Hercules, who's usually shown wielding a wooden club in his right hand, and with a lion's pelt draped over his left. But Hercules is normally depicted with rather less spectacular tackle.

The current thinking is that he's probably a hybrid of Roman Hercules and a native British god whose name we don't know, who might represent strength or fertility. This process of syncretism, blending elements of different faiths together, is a common trait across the Ancient Roman Empire, and is in evidence in the case of the Mother Goddesses, too (page 139).

What we don't know is whether the Giant started off as a Celtic hill figure, and then gained a club and a lion skin to transform into Hercules, or whether he began life as a hybrid under Roman rule sometime between AD 43 (when the Romans invaded) and 410 (when the Romans left).

Further up the hill, above the Giant, is a Bronze Age round barrow (from around 2000 BC) and a rectangular bank-and-ditch earthwork that is probably Iron Age (from 800 BC–AD 43). It's known locally as The Trendle. We don't know what it was used for, but just like the set of monuments and earthworks at Uffington (page 133), the enclosure is surely linked to the position of the Giant. Certainly it indicates that this Dorset hillside has been special for at least 4,000 years. The Trendle is still used for May Day dancing and drinking, and it's entirely possible that this folk tradition has continued unbroken since the creation of the hill figure itself, or perhaps even before.

Just like our other hill figures, his connection to the community is what keeps the Giant alive. If he were to be neglected for even a single generation, he'd no longer exist – grass would grow over the chalk trenches and he'd fade back to green. He now gets re-chalked every ten years by volunteers from around the world. They dig out the old discoloured chalk, then hammer in 17 tonnes of new chalk into the 460 m (1,500 ft) of trench that makes up his outline. Just like our ancestors must have done.

Right The Giant used to have a smaller penis and a cape or animal pelt over his arm. Is he Celtic, Roman, or both?

Maiden Castle

*A hill transformed
into a fortress*

Dorset

Right Maiden Castle is a natural hill, transformed into the most impressive earthwork fortress in Europe. It started off simple, around 600 BC, with just one ring of defences. The vast circuits of ramparts visible now were mostly dug around 100 BC.

This was a busy community, a place of prestige, but it was also a practical stronghold at a time of inter-tribal conflict. It had also been somewhere special for more than 3,000 years already. Britain's earliest farmers cleared the trees on this hilltop, dug two oval circuits of ditches to create a special enclosure, and then a very long 'bank barrow', 550 m (1,800 ft) long, over the hill. Its purpose remains unknown, but the hill's potency endures.

Glastonbury Tor

Ancient mysteries rising from the marshes

Somerset

Left The lonely thirteenth-century tower is the only remaining structure from St Michael's Church.

Wander up Glastonbury's high street and you'll find shops filled with crystals and dream-catchers. You can book a sacred dream tour or learn divination. You can also seek out the paths of local ley lines.

Leys are thought to be channels of energy that extend long distances across the Earth's surface. Believers say they sense these pathways in their bodies, or use dowsing rods to indicate the energy flows as they cross them. No one has yet found a scientific instrument that can measure these forces and interestingly, the person to first coin the term 'ley line' didn't have in mind any mystical potency. Alfred Watkins was a British photographer working in the 1920s. He noted that many ancient sites and notable natural features appeared to be aligned, and these alignments could be seen with the naked eye. Watkins suggested that since prehistoric times people had been crossing the landscape in straight lines. New sites were orientated on these lines, or 'leys', because this was where people walked. The supernatural, energetic elements of ley lines were only introduced much later, with the rise of new mystical religious movements in the late-1960s and 1970s.

By these later practitioners' accounts, Glastonbury is where two lines of energy – the St Michael line and the St Mary line – intersect. One is masculine, the other feminine, and it's said that these energies with equal but opposing forces lead to an unusual sense of harmony.

Glastonbury certainly feels mellow. And mysterious. And the Tor is unequivocally a puzzle. It can be seen for miles in every direction. The hill itself is natural, but the terraces covering its steep faces are not. An illustration from 1670 shows the lower terraces under cultivation, and for a long time it was thought that they were simply 'strip lynchets' – earth steps created in the medieval period so people could plough and plant steep hillsides. But anyone who has made the climb to the summit will agree that the top levels of the hill are not – and never were – land

151

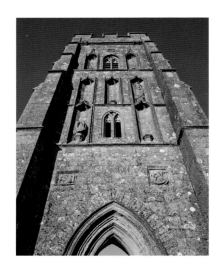

Above Carvings either side of the west doorway show an angel watching an immortal soul be weighed and St Bridget milking a miraculous cow.

suitable for crops. It seems more likely that the terraces are much older, and nothing to do with farming. Most prehistorians think the ancestors terraced the Tor some time around 3000 BC. There's little agreement on why. Did they create the terraces to form a processional route to the top of the hill? Or was the terracing itself the important act? By artificially shaping it, the people transformed a natural feature into a monument. Once altered, it became a special place, a realm of sacred power or magic. Maybe the Tor represents something similar to Silbury Hill (page 125), except the people here didn't have to start from scratch. Either way, the hippies are right – this is not just a hill.

Excavations at the top of the Tor have unearthed various stone tools from the late Stone Age, but nothing that suggests specific ritual activities – no feasting remains, fires or structures. So how they used their supernatural hill remains a mystery. Maybe people paid homage at the bottom of the hill, rather than the top.

Things changed in the sixth century. Here, we find the foundations of timber buildings, evidence of bronze-working and sherds of pottery imported from the Mediterranean. There are also lots of bones from butchered animals and cooked meat. It's an assemblage that you'd expect from a high-status or royal site, like Tintagel (page 173). But there are no gates, walls or defensive circuits. Perhaps it was an early Christian community. But early monks shunned luxuries, including meat-eating. So who were the people feasting and enjoying the fancy Mediterranean imports, but without any need for defences? Here, the evidence eludes us.

By the twelfth century we know a religious community was established at the top of the hill and in a charter from 1243 it's described as 'the monastery of St Michael on the Tor'. The church was destroyed by an earthquake in 1275 but was hastily rebuilt, and the base of the existing tower is from this period.

One complete statue has survived. It's St Dunstan, patron saint of armourers and gunsmiths, and Abbot of Glastonbury in the mid-900s. When St Michael's Church was destroyed in the 1500s during the Dissolution of the Monasteries, Dunstan's statue was spared the zeal of the reformers for some unknown reason. The other details to seek out are the relief carvings either side of the west doorway: an angel looking on as an immortal soul is weighed and, rather more prosaically, St Bridget milking a cow.

The mysterious Tor continued to gather stories throughout the medieval period. Joseph of Arimathea, Jesus' uncle, was said to have taken the cup used at the Last Supper – the Holy Grail – and travelled to Glastonbury, to bury it at the foot of the Tor. Glastonbury's monks promoted this tale to pilgrims coming to worship at the Abbey. Then, following a fire in 1184, the monks revealed another treasure: a lead cross with a Latin inscription. HIC IACET SEPULTUS INCLITUS REX ARTURIUS IN INSULA AVALONIA – 'Here lies buried the renowned King Arthur in the island of Avalon'. A wooden coffin held the remains of a tall man and a small lady, surely King Arthur's beautiful Queen, Guinevere. Compelling evidence, then, that Glastonbury was the holy isle of Avalon, had been visited by a man who'd seen and spoken with Christ and was the last resting place of England's most powerful ancient king. It was fortuitous timing, as the monks badly needed the money to rebuild their burned monastery. Rather conveniently, Arthur's mysterious cross was lost and has yet to be recovered. The unearthed body was reinterred with great fanfare, and you can visit his tomb within the abbey grounds.

The final chapter of the Tor is much darker. In 1539 the elderly Abbot and two of his monks were hung, drawn and quartered on the Tor's church tower, as punishment for concealing some of the abbey's treasures during the Dissolution. The rest of the church was destroyed and the stone reused elsewhere in the town. Now only a lonely tower remains, a beacon rising from the marshes.

Below The hill is natural but the terraces are not. They were probably dug around 3000 BC, during the late Stone Age, perhaps to transform the hill into a monument.

Glastonbury Abbey Lady Chapel

The unfinished chapel of miracles

Somerset

Left In 1184 a huge fire consumed the abbey's ancient timber church and many of the holy relics it contained. Pilgrims visiting the relics were an important source of income for the monastery, so it was decided to rebuild as quickly as possible. King Henry II invested heavily and the new chapel was built in an old-fashioned style designed to make the building feel ancient and mystical. A wooden statue of the Virgin Mary that had apparently (and miraculously) escaped destruction in the fire was installed in the chapel, the statue itself began to perform miracle cures and the pilgrims returned. The north door, pictured, was where most pilgrims entered and is a tour-de-force of mock-Romanesque architecture. After Henry II died in 1189, rebuilding funds dried up and the Abbey faced increasing competition from other pilgrim destinations like Canterbury, where Thomas à Becket had been martyred. The carvings for the chapel's south door weren't yet complete and they remain so to this day, petering out half way down the stonework.

Gough's Cave Cannibal Cup

An Ice Age vessel made from a skull

Somerset

Left The unequivocal evidence that our Ice Age ancestors were doing strange things with dead people's heads.

Britain was still part of continental Europe 14,700 years ago, joined by a vast landmass, Doggerland, which now sits under the North Sea. The weather was generally colder, but for a few months at a time it was warm enough to appeal as a seasonal hunting ground. So small bands of men, women and children travelled north and west and found shelter in natural limestone caves. We now call one of their sites Gough's Cave, in Cheddar Gorge. These people were, evolutionarily, the same as the Red Lady of Paviland Cave (page 177) and you and me – modern *Homo sapiens*. They fashioned tools from flint, bone, wood, antler and mammoth ivory. They hunted horses, hare, grouse and reindeer, and foraged for wild plants, nuts and berries.

They also ate each other.

There are at least six people whose bones were in the cave: two teenagers, a three-year old and three adults – all of them were cut with human tools. Archaeologists have long struggled with the evidence for cannibalism – cut marks on the bones suggested butchery, scalping and filleting, and bones had been chewed and broken apart to reach the insides. But nothing was burned or cooked. Most experts thought that the likeliest explanation was starvation cannibalism – people were eating each other – meat, marrow and brains – out of necessity.

But recent 3D modelling and microscopic analysis of one of these 14,700-year-old arms indicates this behaviour was driven not by hunger but by ritual. One of the adults' right-hand forearms was cut off and the bones filleted out. The end of the radius bone was chewed, and the flat plane was engraved with zigzags. Lastly, it was fractured to access the marrow inside. This was careful and complex behaviour, not a hastily gobbled meal to avoid starvation.

And then there are the skull cups. Archaeologists describe their creation as 'skilled post-mortem processing of the head'. First the head was carefully cut from the body, shortly after death, while the muscles were still fresh.

The jaw was cut away, the tongue, lips, ears and nose detached. Cut marks around and inside the eye sockets suggest the cheeks and eyeballs were removed next. Little cut marks around the hairline indicate the person was then scalped. At some point the maker removed the brain and then carefully chipped away the bone on the edges of the cranial vault to make them as smooth as possible. They transformed the head into a cup.

We don't know what this 'cup' might have been used for. Maybe libations were drunk from it; perhaps it was used to contain something else, or kept pristine. It clearly wasn't just a means of reaching the tasty brain; if you want to get to someone's brain you can just smash their head open. And there are easier ways to hold liquids using gut or skin rather than making cups from skulls.

We don't know who these people were, who were either honoured or desecrated by having their heads turned into cups. Were they members of the tribe, enemies or strangers? Did people come to Gough's Cave specifically to

perform these rituals, or did they just happen to be here when the people died? There's no evidence on the bones we have that these people were intentionally killed, but then most deaths don't make a mark on the bones.

There are plenty of cross-cultural examples of people using human skulls as special vessels. Herodotus says the Scythians did it, Sima Qian says the Chinese did it, Magnus Olafsson says the Vikings did it, and we have more recent ethnographic evidence from India, Australia and Fiji. For some cultures, you'd drink from the skull of your enemy to demonstrate your power and their obliteration; for others, you drink from the skulls of people you revere or love to honour them.

Modern funeral practices may seem as odd to the Gough's Cave people as their craft and cannibalism does to us. Mutilation or magic – what better way to keep the spirit of the dead alive than by consuming them? You are, after all, what you eat.

Below A 14,700-year-old human arm bone that was chewed by a person, split to reach the marrow, and carefully engraved with zigzags.

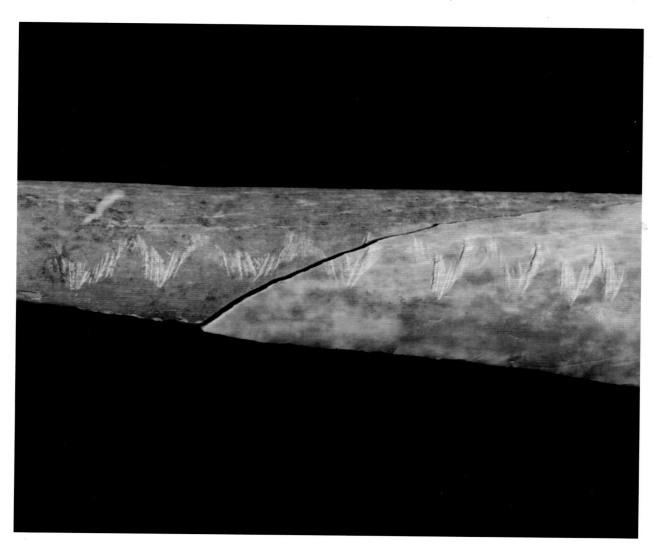

Dartmoor

Stone rows and secret circles in a lost land

Devon

Left Shovel Down boasts a stone
circle, cairns, multiple stone rows
and an enormous standing stone
known as the Longstone.
Next page The stunning complex
of monuments and hut circles at
Merrivale are some of the finest
in Dartmoor and were in use for
more than a thousand years.

Remote and windswept, surely human activity has made little mark
on this land of bottomless bog, weather-blasted granite and strange
curling mists. It's almost 1,000 km² (385 square miles) of wild, open
land, but in fact, Dartmoor is very much a landscape forged by
human hands, and it boasts more than 20,000 archaeological sites
to prove it. The first people here arrived at the end of the Ice Age,
hunting and gathering in the wildwoods and along the rivers, but
the real changes were made by the first farmers, some 6,000 years
ago, when they started to cut down the trees to create open land for
crops and grazing.

To really time travel you need to imagine a patchwork landscape
of native, wizened oaks and scrubby vegetation, clearings and tracks,
fast-moving water courses and the sculptural forms of the granite
outcrops known as 'tors'. Just a few slivers of the native wildwood still
exist, like Wistman's Wood and Blackator Copse, where the trees are
hung with lichen and it feels as though you're entering a fairy grotto.
Most of the peat beds on Dartmoor hadn't formed yet, so erase the
thick black bogs, mossy wastes and rough tussocks – they come later.
Neolithic farmers began the deforestation with a cycle of clearing,
burning and grazing, and by 1700 BC during the Bronze Age, much
of Dartmoor's forest was gone. More people lived on Dartmoor at this
point than at any time before or since. Dartmoor was a busy place. You
can find the remains of animal enclosures, field boundaries, ritual
sites and the homes of these early farmers. Head to a spot on the map
labelled 'hut circles' in curly gothic script, and you'll find low rings
of stones with gaps on the southern sides. Step over the threshold,
and you're in the house of someone who was alive more than 3,000
years ago. These homes may well have had similar cosmological and
practical organisation as the roundhouses in the Hebrides (see Cladh

Above Down Tor stone row stretches more than 300 m (980 ft) before reaching the tall terminal pillar, pictured, and a stone circle surrounding a central cairn.

Hallan, page 299), where people may have moved 'sunwise' (clockwise) around a central hearth and the elements of the house represented the elements of the universe.

Even though we can piece together some elements of these ancient lives, other aspects defy interpretation. The most baffling archaeological sites are the stone rows. We now know about seventy-five stone rows on Dartmoor, and it's likely that there are more undiscovered rows hidden in peat beds, waiting to be unearthed. The shortest, at Merrivale, is less than 3 m (10 ft) long – and the longest, Stallmoor Stone Row, is more than 3.3 km (2 miles). It's the longest prehistoric line of stones in the world.

Stone rows are formed from single lines, pairs of stones and, more rarely, triple rows of stone, like at Cosdon Hill. Sometimes, they link other monuments like standing stones, burial mounds and stone circles. Other times, they appear to sit in strange isolation, starting and stopping in the middle of otherwise empty moorland. They're not consistent enough to have been used as territorial markers. Boundaries between different farming families were marked by earthen banks known as reaves, which you can still spot forging across the landscape, low and resolutely straight, overlaid with a depth of peat that indicates their ancient age. Dartmoor's stone rows are clearly different – perhaps they're boundary stones that demarcate sacred landscapes rather than everyday functional ones, or markers for some kind of ceremonial route. They don't appear to help with astronomical observations, but maybe our modern eyes are looking for the wrong things. Perhaps they were ways to tell stories about the landscape. Or maybe the construction of the row was more important than the finished product (perhaps in the same way rock art may have been made and used, see Ilkley Moor, page 53).

Stone rows are also hard to date, but we can glean some evidence from examining the remnants found at the bottom of the socket holes into which the stones have been placed. It appears that the earliest rows were possibly erected in the middle Neolithic, from around 3500 BC, but they were also used – and reused – in the Bronze Age from 2400–1500 BC.

The most elaborate monumental complexes, for example those at Merrivale, Drizzlecombe and Shovel Down, are a dizzying arrangement of rows, cairns and monoliths. Some of the elements feel connected, others stand apart. But we may be looking at a puzzle with missing pieces, or something of a work-in-progress that was never finished.

People continued to farm Dartmoor until around 1000 BC, when the weather grew cooler and wetter and peat started to form on areas that had previously been fertile. Farmers found their margins for growing enough food were shrinking, and grain that was harvested might rot as readily as it might be successfully stored. Eventually they moved away, and busy villages turned into lonely clusters of archaeological 'hut circles'.

Dartmoor can feel like a mysterious place now, haunted by hell hounds, miry spirits and these strange stones speaking messages we no longer understand. And yet the Dartmoor that people built these monuments on was a rich and fertile place, full of life and livestock. Theirs was not a wild and windswept land, it was – to a greater or lesser extent – a bucolic idyll. As metal-working was introduced to Britain, the people of Dartmoor thrived. They panned for the cassiterite tin ores they found in the streams and rivers, and were able to trade it widely – tin is an essential component of bronze.

These communities didn't grow to be regional powers; they stayed small and independent, and in Roman times, the reputation of the fiercely proud people still living in this area meant the conquerors left them well alone. That same fierce liberty endures in Dartmoor today. This landscape may be shaped by human hands, but it certainly hasn't been tamed.

Below Drizzlecombe teases with possible patterns – large cairns lead to single, and sometimes partly double stone rows, that then terminate in substantial standing stones.

Trethevy Quoit

A portal to the gods

Cornwall

This teetering stack is known locally as the Giant's House. Its old Cornish name, Trethevy, means 'The Place of the Graves'. Both names might contain some truth: even though no human remains have ever been found here, we're pretty clear that it was used for burial rites. But it was also probably used for a lot more.

Trethevy is a type of monument known as a 'dolmen'. They're also known as a *cromlech* in Wales, or *quoit* in this stretch of western Cornwall. Dolmens were built around 3700–3300 BC, during the middle of the late Stone Age or Neolithic era. Like many other dolmens, Trethevy is on high ground, but not at a summit. Instead, it sits on the south-eastern side of a low hill, aligned east–west, overlooking a confluence of streams that flow from wellsprings to the River Seaton.

The stones are local granite, arranged to form a main chamber and a small entrance area. Overlapping slabs form the sides, and at the front, eastern end, is a standing stone with a narrow notch cut out of the bottom corner. This stone is at right angles to the others, acting like a door, restricting access to the inner part of the structure. Many dolmens have this feature, known as a portal stone, alongside flanking stones that create an antechamber or forecourt. The stone at the back of the Trethevy dolmen has dropped inwards and now rests inside the chamber. The fall of this end stone is probably the reason the 20 tonne capstone is tilted so sharply; it's credit to the Stone Age builders that the collapse of one stone didn't spell disaster for the whole monument.

It's the capstone that's the most striking aspect of any dolmen. They're always much larger than you'd need to simply create a roof. At some sites, like Pentre Ifan (pictured on page 168), the capstone soars, perfectly balanced on its uprights. At others, like Chûn Quoit (page 169) , it feels like the rock has been prised from the earth just high enough to create a space underneath.

Below Pentre Ifan in Pembrokeshire is a masterpiece of prehistoric construction. The uprights delicately balance the 16-tonne capstone 2.5 m (8 ft 2 in) above the ground. A mysterious portal stone stands at right angles between the uprights on the left.

The small rocks embedded in the soil around the Trethevy dolmen are the remains of a cairn. We don't know whether the cairn completely covered the dolmen, or whether it formed a ring around it, possibly heaped up around its sides. Recent excavations suggest that the top of the capstone was just as important as the space inside, intended to remain in view, raised up and held between the sky above and the dark chamber below. Maybe they were used as giant stone altars, or platforms for sky burial, or excarnation, where dead bodies would be laid out until the flesh rotted away and the bones picked clean by animals or birds. Some of the bones could have been collected to go inside the dolmen, others would be left to disperse. Maybe living members of the tribe were sometimes expected to go beyond the portal and into the chamber, perhaps during initiation or other rituals. And when there were human remains inside the

chamber, the primary aim might not have been to bury them, but to put them in a house.

Perhaps dolmens were places for the whole community. Imagine a parish church in a modern Christian community – it's surrounded by graves, but if we only described it as a mortuary monument, we'd misrepresent its purpose and its community. It's also used for coffee mornings, harvest festivals, weddings and baptisms. It's both a space and an idea, where individuals might become part of something beyond themselves, and where the dead are both bodily, and spiritually, present. That's how we should think about dolmens: places of community, identity, death and transformation.

Below **Chûn Quoit in Cornwall sits on high ground overlooking the sea, surrounded by the remains of a cairn. We don't know if the cairn fully covered the dolmen, or whether the stones were always in view.**

Men an Tol

A place of wishes

Cornwall

Right The name means 'stone with a hole' in Cornish and the site is probably about 4,000 years old, dating to the Bronze Age. There are more stones hidden under the turf, and it's been suggested that the visible stones have been moved and were never originally designed to be in a line.

Legends and folktales linger here – crawl through the Holed Stone and your longing for a baby will be rewarded, or pass your baby through the stone, and you'll protect them from rickets, consumption, or fever. This strange portal promises a safer future, from a timeless past.

Tintagel

King Arthur's island of stories

Cornwall

Left The Earl of Cornwall built a real castle that could pass as the location for the exploits of legendary heroes and heroines. Tintagel is a medieval Neverland.

Tintagel is almost an island – surrounded by sea but linked to the main Cornish coast by an increasingly slim strip of rock and sand. It's like the set of a Hollywood showstopper, steeped in myth, a perfect backdrop for tales of knights and damsels from a lost age. The archaeological reality is a little more nuanced, but just as stunning.

The name 'Tintagel' originates from early Cornish, with *din* meaning 'fort' (similar to *dùn* in Scotland) and *tagell* meaning 'neck of land'. The island and the main coastline were, until some point in the 1500s, joined by a land bridge wide enough to be built upon, but a series of landslides has rendered it even more dramatically inaccessible now than it was in antiquity.

There's not much evidence for human activity on Tintagel from the Roman period, but from about AD 450–650 it became a place of wealth and power, with the remains of at least 100 buildings surviving and a large defensive ditch that you can still see. Most significantly, excavators found the remains of pottery amphorae used to store olive oil and wine, fancy red-and-black tableware and glassware from southern Spain. The amphorae were imported from modern-day Turkey, Greece, Tunisia and Syria, and excavations at Tintagel have yielded more of this kind of imported pottery than anywhere else in Britain, so it was clearly somewhere special.

Indeed, it seems very likely that Tintagel was one of the royal residences for the kings of the joint kingdom of Devon and Cornwall. Although the collapse of Roman rule in Britain left some places in total disarray, it seems like the leaders here took advantage of new opportunities for trade and political connection. Luxury food and tablewares were imported and consumed, tin and perhaps slaves were exported and the people controlling this trade grew rich. We don't know if Tintagel was just one of many seasonal royal residences, or

Above Tintagel became even more dramatically inaccessible when a series of landslides in the 1500s lost most of the land bridge that originally joined it to the main coast.

whether it had a specific role. An intriguing clue exists at the top of the island – what appears to be a footprint cut into the rock. It's just like the one at Dunadd in western Scotland (page 225) and it might suggest that Tintagel was a site for royal inauguration; a place where kings were made.

It's perhaps an oral memory of this history that provoked the twelfth-century cleric, Geoffrey of Monmouth, to name Tintagel in his book, *The History of the Kings of Britain*, as the place where King Arthur was conceived. Alongside historically real kings, Geoffrey wrote about the legendary leaders of the nation too, including the Roman Brutus who defeats the giants to found Britain, and King Arthur.

Stories about Arthur were already popular currency; fantasy versions of what were probably episodes from one or more real leaders' biographies. Throughout the medieval period, versions of Arthur's story proliferated, and later stories make Tintagel the place where Arthur is born too, and home of his court of knights.

In May 1233, Richard, Earl of Cornwall, brother of King Henry III, went to great lengths to acquire the island of 'Tyntagel'. The headland was no longer a strategic or military asset, but Richard was ambitious, and owning Tintagel presented an opportunity to put himself at the heart of a legend.

As well as Arthur, there's another medieval tale that has strong links to Tintagel and was just as popular in Earl Richard's time: the tragic love story of Tristan and Iseult. In the tale, heroic Tristan escorts beautiful Iseult from Ireland to his uncle, King Mark of Cornwall, at his royal castle on Tintagel. Mark and Iseult intend to marry, but on the journey she and Tristan take a love potion (in some versions accidentally, in others, intentionally) and fall in love with one another instead. When they reach Tintagel, Iseult marries Mark but continues her affair with Tristan, romancing in the halls and gardens of their island home. Eventually Mark finds out about their treachery and sentences his wife and nephew to death. But Tristan escapes by jumping out of a cliff-top chapel. He gallops to rescue his beloved Iseult, they flee to safety in a forest and shelter in a cave. In the final chapter of the tale they broker peace with Mark on the provision that Iseult returns to Ireland and Tristan is banished to France. In short, the pair do not live happily ever after, but it's terribly romantic and exciting along the way.

Richard made the world of these fictional characters real. He built a castle that would serve for Mark, the fictional King of Cornwall, and for himself, the new Earl of Cornwall. He constructed a romantic walled garden on the wind-blasted plateau and a hand-carved grotto that could be the lovers' hideout that Tristan and Iseult use in the forest. And perhaps most compellingly, a chapel was built at the very edge of the clifftop (and oddly out of sync from the main castle buildings). The eastern wall teeters over dramatic cliffs, just like the chapel that Tristan leaps from at the climax of his tale.

We don't know whether, once built, fact and fiction blended, so that visitors to Tintagel were encouraged to believe that this really was the place these heroes and heroines had lived, or whether it was acknowledged as an imaginative and entertaining fantasy. Much like today, where people are drawn to visit Hogwarts, or Juliet's balcony, they're compelled by the story, rather than the truth.

Tintagel castle certainly wasn't built to high military standards. Within a decade some of the buildings were unstable, and in contemporary reports, the Great Hall was recorded as being 'ruinous' in 1337, just a hundred years after it was built. Tintagel isn't a castle for war, it's a castle for stories.

Below Between AD 450–650 Tintagel was a wealthy and important place. Far from being a barrier, the sea was a highway for traders who had networks reaching as far as Spain, Greece and Syria.

Paviland Cave Burial

The blood-red dust staining a 33,000-year-old burial

South Wales

Left Paviland Cave sits half way up jagged cliffs. 33,000 years ago it overlooked a wide, dry plain. This is the site of the earliest known human burial in Britain.

Red ochre is an earth pigment that occurs naturally, and commonly, throughout the world, including in Britain. It's been found on archaeological sites from South Africa to Australia. It's iron oxide – more commonly known as rust – and it's been found on shells, cave walls and in human burials that span thousands of years.

The earliest intentional human burial found in Britain, the so-called 'Red Lady' of Paviland, was discovered in 1823 in a teardrop-shaped cave in a cliff in south-west Wales. The bones, actually those of a young man who died during the last Ice Age, have been radiocarbon dated to a staggering 33,000 years old. And they're stained with red ochre. Originally, the powdered ochre must have been on the man's body or clothes, and as the flesh rotted away, the pigment naturally transferred to the bones left in the grave and the perforated periwinkle shells he was wearing as beads. Many other burials discovered from this period elsewhere in Europe also have ochre in the grave – daubed on jewellery, clothes and bodies, particularly around the head and feet. In one woman's grave from El Mirón cave in Spain, it looks like people dug the body or bones up again to re-ochre the remains, before reburying them.

You'll also recognise ochre from prehistoric cave painting. Spat over ancient human hands, to create visceral stencils, or carefully mixed with water or fat, and painted into bison, horse and giant cattle that stream across the rocks, red and alive.

But these Ice Age humans weren't the first people to use this pigment. Evidence of collecting and using ochre goes back some 300,000 years, by *Homo erectus* in Kenya, and 200,000 years by our cousins *Homo neanderthalensis* in the Netherlands. There are also engraved and ochred bones from a 100,000-year-old site in China used by our other archaic cousins, *Homo denisova*.

Use by these early human species might indicate that ochre didn't start off symbolic or artistic. It might have been functional and only became ritualised much later. Experimental archaeology and ethnographic study of modern hunter-gatherer peoples reveals that there are plenty of mundane uses for this strange dust. Rub it onto meat and it lasts longer, and deters carnivores from stealing it. Rub it on yourself, and it masks your scent from animals you're hunting. It also works as an insect repellent, a sunscreen and an antiseptic to prevent wounds getting infected. It's useful in tanning hides and making compound glues. It's an all-purpose product for the hunter-gatherer about town.

But why was it in the burial at Paviland Cave? The cave now overlooks wild rocks that are inundated with every tide, but when the man was buried, they overlooked a vast dry plain that stretched far into

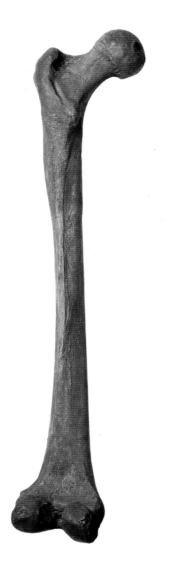

what's now the Bristol Channel. It teemed with game and other wild resources that he and his hunter-gatherer group lived on. They would have travelled widely, following the herds, moving with the seasons. The ochre and periwinkle shells could have been collected by them as they travelled, or exchanged with other bands of Ice Age people. The population of Britain during this time was probably no more than a couple of hundred, surviving in a hostile environment with skills finessed over generations. But life wasn't just hand-to-mouth. These people were as intellectually and emotionally complex as we are – so when this young man died, he was treated carefully and ceremonially.

He was buried in a cave, half way up a cliff. He was covered in ochre, wore shell ornaments and had stone and bone tools and numerous tiny cylinders of mammoth ivory. These could be blanks for bead-making, or they could be some kind of finished artefact in their own right. We don't know what, though, and there's no immediately obvious way to use them. If they were bead-making materials, why would they be buried with him, rather than taken and used by someone else? Mammoth ivory is time-consuming to craft and rare enough to be precious, so abandoning the raw material must have been a significant act. Perhaps the ivory became unlucky when he died, or he needed it in the afterlife. We only have parts of the man's skeleton, and what we do have doesn't offer any clues as to how this young man died. Maybe the nature of his death determined how his body was treated in the grave. Perhaps the ochre was an honour, or maybe it was a balm, to make a bad death less bad. Or maybe it was just normal – ochre was an everyday thing.

Either way, we should remember that being functional doesn't reduce an item's capacity to be spiritual. Even if it's a common substance, it can still be potent – compare holy offerings of bread in the Christian tradition, rice among Hindus or lamp oil in a Jewish temple. There's also something special about red. Almost every existing human language has a word for 'red'. Languages with just two colour-based words will have black and white, and if there's a third colour distinction it is always, without fail, red. It's exciting, dangerous and important. It's the colour of blood – and therefore both life and death, which makes colouring a corpse red, like the young man of Paviland, a profoundly transformative act. So even if ochre makes a good sunscreen or lion-deterrant, its appeal will surely have also stemmed from its colour.

Most of the things our British ancestors coloured red – their skin, their beads, their bones, their rocks – will never be seen by us. The pigment washes away almost as easily as it is applied, and 30,000 years and an Ice Age can do some hefty damage to archaeological remains. But if you ever stumble across an outcrop or nodule of red ochre, take a minute to appreciate the beauty of the blood dust. Rub it on your skin and transport yourself into the world of the ancestors.

Kilpeck Sheela Na Gig

The X-rated woman leering from a church

Herefordshire

Left Large staring eyes, no hair and no clothes. And she's grabbing open her genitalia. On a church.

The whole of the Church of St Mary and St David in Kilpeck, Herefordshire is a wonder. It was built around 1140, probably commissioned by a Norman lord returning from crusade in the Holy Land. There are the quintessential architectural details of a 'Romanesque' church, like rounded doorways decorated with chevrons and beak-heads (characters that bite the circuit of masonry they're carved into) and a semi-circular apse at the eastern end where the altar is. But Kilpeck is also covered in elaborate, characterful carvings: there are dragons, angels, griffins and green men, and intricate celtic knotwork.

It's outside near the roof that you'll see the strangest carvings. On the corbels (bracket-shaped supports on the walls), there are creatures and characters apparently representing virtues and sins. A dog that looks like Snoopy is 'faithfulness'. He sits next to a hare that might be 'fear of god'. There are two little birds biting a snake, a pig eating a person, someone playing the fiddle and a man pinching someone's bottom. And on the south-eastern side of the apse, there's a leering woman reaching between her legs and holding her labia apart. This is a sheela na gig. She has large staring eyes, isn't wearing any clothes and doesn't seem to have any hair. Other sheelas have sagging breasts, their ribs showing or scars cut across their cheeks.

The interpretations are varied – perhaps she represents lust, demonstrating the evils of the world compared to the sanctity and refuge of the church. She might be a temptation, designed to tempt church-goers to have a peek, and then realise how easy it is to fall from grace.

It's difficult to decide whether an image from another culture or time is supposed to be appealing, but to a modern eye a sheela often looks more scary than sexy. Maybe she's also there to frighten away

the devil. The final theory is that she's a fertility symbol that survived from pagan times into Christian imagery. Many of the carvings on Kilpeck Church symbolise life and death in some way – so maybe she's revealing the visceral nature of birth, fertility and perhaps the inevitability of ageing.

Over the years, many sheelas have been destroyed by people distressed by the x-rated woman on their church. But the remarkable thing about Kilpeck is that, mostly, no one has changed much of anything. That's why we have such an architectural gem on our hands. But we do have evidence that some of the Kilpeck corbels were chiselled away in relatively recent times, allegedly on instruction from the vicar's wife. She didn't mind the sheela, so what did she object to? A corbel from St John's Church in Devizes, Wiltshire, might give us a clue. It has two figures next to one another – one is a sheela and the other is a man masturbating his large, erect penis. Maybe that's what we're missing from Kilpeck.

Left Kilpeck Church was built around 1140 and little changed since then. It's a masterpiece of Norman Romanesque architecture.
Below A green man figure on the southern door, with plants growing from his mouth. Medieval church carving often seems rather 'pagan' to modern eyes, but this figure might also represent the word of God spreading into the world.

Preseli Bluestones

The missing link to Stonehenge

Pembrokeshire

Left Careful examination of the outcrop at Carn Goedog will reveal where stone pillars have been prised away, as well as stones cleaved off but then abandoned.

You'll find two main types of stone at Stonehenge (page 115). The largest stones are made of sarsen, a type of sandstone found in Wiltshire, within a day's walk of the monument. The others, which make up the smaller circle within the henge, are from south-west Wales. They're not all the same kind of stone – there's spotted dolerite, rhyolite and sandstones among others – but together they're referred to as bluestones, because of their colour. These Welsh stones are dwarfed by the sarsens, but they're still massive – up to 3 m (10 ft) tall and weighing as much as an elephant.

For a long time archaeologists have speculated on the exact origins of these stones, and why they were selected to be included in the great henge of Salisbury Plain. We've known since the 1920s that they were from somewhere in the Preseli Hills in Pembrokeshire, but it's only in the last decade that geological testing has been able to pinpoint the origins of an individual stone. The technique the experts used is laser ablation inductively coupled plasma mass spectrometry, which involves 'ablating' (vaporising) crystals in the rock and analysing their chemical makeup. At least one of the rhyolite bluestones (along with 1,200 loose stone chippings found in the ground at Stonehenge) is from the outcrop of Craig Rhos-y-felin, and the majority of spotted dolerite stones were quarried from Carn Goedog.

Carn Goedog is a striking place; as you climb uphill, the teeth of rock are silhouetted against a wide sky. The dolerite naturally forms into pillar shapes, which split easily. Excavation at the site suggests that the people quarrying the stone looked for natural lines of weakness, drove wooden wedges into the cracks and then let the wood swell with water in order to gently ease each pillar away. The jury is still out on how the stones were then moved more than 200 km (125 miles) to Stonehenge. The most likely theories are either that they were taken overland on wooden sleds or dragged to the river and floated on rafts

Below Was this area, now remote and rural, once an important and influential spiritual centre?

downstream for part of the journey and then dragged overland the rest of the way.

Some of the stones at Carn Goedog have a 'ringing' property. If you tap them with a smaller stone, they'll resonate deeply and melodically, and it's possible that this is part of their appeal. You can still find ringing stones within the outcrop as well as lying on the ground nearby. But trying to get into the mindset of people from some 5,000 years ago is hardly straightforward. It could have been colour, acoustics, location or something entirely abstract that made these stones special.

The spiked rockfaces at Craig Rhos-y-Felin are no less remarkable than those at Carn Goedog. You round the corner of a winding woodland road, ford the river and then you see the stone. It's natural, yet somehow architectural. It feels otherworldly; a place of significance.

Just like at Carn Goedog, the natural weaknesses in rock were exploited so that obelisk-shaped pieces could be prised off. In some places you can even spot the stump from where a rock has been removed, and there's one great rock lying flat on the ground, as if ready to go. For whatever reason, the people went to all the effort of quarrying this particular stone, but then didn't remove it. It's now fully exposed, but when archaeologists first discovered it, it was hidden by soil that had washed down from the slope above.

And there's even more intrigue. We can't directly date the time these stones were moved or shaped, but we can get dates from materials found in conjunction to the quarrying. Excavators discovered charcoal and burnt hazelnut shells in what might have been the workers' campfires. They were radiocarbon dated to around 3500–2900 BC for Craig Rhos-y-felin, and 3350–3000 BC for Carn Goedog. We think the bluestones were first erected at Stonehenge around 3000 BC, in the Aubrey holes.

This might mean there's unaccounted time between the stones being quarried and their use at Stonehenge. The reason the dates aren't more accurate is because the radiocarbon calibration curve at this point in prehistory is flat, so each result has a wider possible date range.

If the earlier dates are correct, where were the stones for those centuries between that first quarrying and their final journey to Wiltshire?

Our best guess is that some or all of these stones started off as a monument elsewhere. There's no evidence at the quarry sites that suggests the stones were erected there, which means the original monument sites for the bluestones are still out there waiting to be found. There are hundreds of prehistoric sites preserved in the valleys and uplands around Preseli, including burial cairns and stone circles, but what we're looking for is the most elusive of prehistoric monuments – the one that is no longer there.

More confusingly, we can only account for one Craig Rhos-y-felin stone reaching Stonehenge. What happened to the others? Perhaps they were lost in transit, or used in a different monument that's since been destroyed. Or they may survive somewhere, hidden under ancient soil, waiting to be rediscovered. Given the importance of these stones to the builders of Stonehenge, and the communities in Preseli who quarried them, they may be the single most important class of Neolithic sites we don't have.

Intriguingly, the isotope analysis of human remains from around Stonehenge has shown that a number of people buried at the site grew up in west Wales and travelled between the two places – the distinctive geology leaves a chemical signature in their teeth. So there was a clear link between the community living in Wiltshire and the people of Preseli.

The Preseli Hills are sparsely populated now, but it's possible that this was an important area during Neolithic times, perhaps a centre of spiritual influence or sacred nature gods. More research may reveal details that will help us piece together the logistics of these stone-moving activities, but the deeper mysteries of the bluestones may remain tantalisingly out of reach.

Penbryn Spoons

Enigmatic tools to divine the future

Ceredigion

Right One spoon boasts a hole by the rim. The other is scored with a cross and four inlaid dots. The most convincing explanation for these strange objects is that they were used in fortune-telling rituals.

These hand-sized cast bronze 'spoon-like objects' are around 2,000 years old. They were found in 1829 carefully buried under a pile of stones inside Castell Nadolig, or 'Christmas Castle', an Iron Age hillfort in Penbryn in west Wales. They weren't everyday tools: these are mystic spoons.

Only twenty-three other spoons like these have ever been discovered, and apart from one pair in France, they've only ever been found in Britain and Ireland. All but three were found in pairs, and it's thought that the three singles probably had a lost mate.

Each of the Penbryn spoons has a decorated stub handle so you can hold it between forefinger and thumb. And just like all the other mysterious paired spoons, one of them has a hole drilled through the bowl, while the other is engraved with two lines that form a cross through the centre. If you look closely, you'll see spots on the cross-incised spoon. These were originally inlaid with different metals, including one of gold. This inlay is a unique decoration among all the mystic spoons we have.

The prevailing theory is that these spoons were used for divination, by dripping or blowing a thick liquid (like oil or blood) or very fine powder through the 'hole spoon' into the 'cross spoon'. The diviner would read the pattern and foretell the future or reveal the gods' desires. Like reading tea leaves, or the Roman practice of reading the entrails of a sacrificed animal, the truth is laid out in an otherwise random pattern. Divination could have been used to foretell when to commence battle or raiding, or for auspicious times to plant crops, marry or travel.

The spoons are easily portable, so could have travelled with a roving priest or priestess. Or they could be linked to Castell Nadolig hillfort itself rather than to a specific individual. The Penbryn spoons weren't in association with a dead body, although three other pairs of ritual spoons have been found in graves: one pair in Deal, Kent, were placed on either side of the dead person's head; the pair from Pogny, France, were found one inside the other in a bag under an upturned bronze bowl on top of a dead woman's right arm; and the pair in Burnmouth, Berwick, were placed in a man's grave in front of his face along with pieces of coal, an iron knife and the bones of a young pig.

Spoons were deposited from the middle to the late Iron Age, around 300 BC–AD 100. Julius Caesar, who wrote extensively about the religious and ritual practices of the native peoples of Britain and Gaul, describes Iron Age druids counting time not by the number of days, but by the number of nights. He says the Gauls used calendars that measured the four phases of the waxing, waning, new or full moon. Maybe the answers these spoons offered were linked to this world view. Maybe the quartered spoons represent moon time.

Bryn Cader Faner

A wild circle of thorns

Gwynedd

Left Fifteen tall, slim stones spread outwards, silhouetted like a crown of thorns: this is a 3,500-year-old burial monument known as a ring cairn, with a stone circle surrounding a ring of heaped stones. We don't know whether the cairn came first or the circle, or whether they were constructed at the same time. The depression at the centre is where a stone-lined box was positioned, containing a burial or cremation. It was dug up in the 1800s and any remains and artefacts were lost at the hands of the treasure hunters. It's a 7-km (4½-mile) walk across wild upland to reach this place. It's worth every windswept step.

Tre'r Ceiri

*Windswept rooms
with a view*

Gwynedd

Right On a windswept peak of
Yr Eifl, on the Llŷn Peninsula in
north Wales, sits an astonishingly
preserved prehistoric village.
Unlike other hillforts, such
as Maiden Castle (page 142),
the arresting features aren't
the ramparts, but the houses
within. There are more than 150
prehistoric homes to visit. Walk
in the footsteps of the ancestors:
up past cultivation terraces and
animal enclosures, in through
the village entrance and up to
someone's front door. Imagine
simple furniture, a central hearth
and a smoky pall hanging below
the thatched roof. Home to a
thriving community in the Iron
Age and throughout the Roman
occupation, Tre'r Ceiri survived
because people liked living here.

Barclodiad y Gawres and Bryn Celli Ddu

Magical tombs of otherworldly decoration

Anglesey

Left The burial mound of Bryn Celli Ddu, which translates as 'Mound in the Dark Grove'. This has been a special site for at least 8,000 years.

Next page The swirling designs of the Pattern Stone are more commonly found on tombs in Ireland, Brittany and Portugal. This stone was never designed to be visible – it was originally laid flat and buried under the mound. This replica is on site – the original is protected from erosion at the National Museum Wales.

Step inside the passage tomb at Bryn Celli Ddu and you enter a realm that should not be seen by the living. Stand with your back to the wall and look east down the passage towards the rising sun. In the shadows on your left, allow the darkness to resolve into a vaguely human-shaped figure. It's actually a pillar of stone, intentionally smoothed, and positioned in the corner of the tomb that's never lit from outside. But it feels like more than just a rock: it feels like a guardian, perhaps, or a demon. For many centuries, local people regarded this as a place of spirits, somewhere not to be meddled with. It's easy to see why.

The people who built Bryn Celli Ddu, some time between 3074–2956 BC, began by erecting an arc of stones around a central pit or post. Under these arc stones they placed handfuls of ashes from cremations. Then they built the passage and main tomb chamber. They dug an encircling ditch, and used the soil to create a small mound over the top, not much bigger than the size we can see today. A later phase of building work extended the mound and moved the arc stones. Since then, the mound has been depleted, but the wide circle of kerbstones show its initial reach.

The passage itself is perfectly aligned for Midsummer sunrise, when the sun casts a golden beam into the centre of the tomb, lighting up what otherwise feels very much like a shadow zone, far from the surface world.

We can confidently say this is a burial monument, but there isn't much bone to show for it. Piles of bones inside the tomb are described in early reports by visitors to Anglesey, but many of these remains were removed and then misplaced before modern archaeologists could get their hands on them. From the bones we can date, it appears the tomb was actively used as a burial site for the community for a relatively short period of time – between 5 and 182 years.

Above The carved stones at Barclodiad y Gawres are the only other place in Britain we find these rock art motifs. Were these tombs actually built by overseas visitors to Anglesey?

The relationship between the sunrise and a tomb of the dead is intriguing. In the world of subsistence farming, you might be only one bad harvest away from disaster. Was Midsummer an occasion to pray for a successful harvest? Or maybe the sunshine alignment wasn't for the living community at all, but designed to nourish the dead.

Just behind the tomb, on the side opposite the entrance, is a standing stone. It's an exact replica of the original, which now lives indoors in the National Museum of Wales in Cardiff. Both wide faces are covered in zigzagging, psychedelic designs that circuit around each other like contour lines on a map. The stone was part of the first phase of building, with the central pit and the arc of stones. But – and this is the weird thing – right from the beginning, this stone didn't stand upright like it does today. It was carefully carved, laid flat in the pit and then buried under the earth mound. No living eyes were ever supposed to see it. Why not, is anyone's guess.

The name Bryn Celli Ddu means 'Mound in the Dark Grove'. We don't know how long it has had this name, and there are certainly no trees nearby now. It's a useful reminder that natural features we can no longer perceive may have profoundly affected our ancestors' use and interpretation of a site.

In the landscape surrounding the tomb are outcrops of rock covered in cupmarks, ritual carvings that we continue to struggle to explain. They do indicate that this is a spiritual landscape. And the most recent set of radiocarbon dates from this site have revealed a whole extra chapter of interest: tiny samples of pine charcoal were found in a line of post holes in front of the main tomb entrance. The results were staggering – these wooden posts, aligned to the sun, were erected some time between 6000–5700 BC. This is deep in the Mesolithic, the middle Stone Age, before pottery, farming or herding. The astonishing results mean that we know for sure that people have been coming to this spot to mark Midsummer sunrise for at least 8,000 years.

Barclodiad y Gawres is 18 km (11 miles) west of Bryn Celli Ddu. It sits on a dramatic promontory on the Anglesey's west coast, looking over the sea to Ireland. Again, it's a passage grave: a wide forecourt leads to a passage, which leads to a central chamber. This time the chamber is cross-shaped with three side cells. On the large stones that form the junction of the passage and chamber, and at the back of the side chambers are stones decorated with the same swirling, dramatic designs that cover the pattern stone at Bryn Celli Ddu.

We don't see other examples of this kind of rock art in this kind of tomb anywhere else in Britain. The tombs like these are found in Ireland – at Newgrange and Knowth – and Brittany in France and in

Portugal. The other tombs on Anglesey, and elsewhere in North Wales, are portal dolmen tombs (like the ones found in Cornwall, page 167).

The most obvious explanation is that our two passage tombs were built by people from Ireland, France or Portugal. Why this particular style of monument didn't take off is unknown. Maybe the immigrants came, but left again. Maybe they stayed but died out. Or maybe they integrated with local communities and gave up their original building style and beliefs. Or perhaps it was local people who returned from trading trips with new ideas for tomb architecture, convinced enough people to try it, but the exotic experiment didn't pay off.

Below The smooth pillar within Bryn Celli Ddu stands in the shadowy corner that never sees daylight. Is it a tomb guardian? A phallic symbol? Or a representative of the ancestors or spirits?

Mold
Gold Cape

A golden masterpiece

Flintshire

In 1833 workmen were in a field called Bryn yr Ellyllon ('Goblins' Hill'). They were digging for stone and hit a skeleton surrounded by large patterned fragments of very thin sheet gold. They didn't know it, but this grave was some 3,500 years old, containing one of the most unique artefacts in world prehistory. The workmen and the farmer shared out the gold between them, took some of the bones as novelties, and threw the rest away.

A local vicar wrote about the find, and the British Museum arranged to buy the largest piece of gold from the farmer, and other smaller pieces from the workmen. The gold was dated to the Bronze Age (2500–800 BC) but for a long time, the experts thought that they'd bought a fancy piece of horse harness decoration. It was only in the 1960s that conservators were able to complete the 3D jigsaw and work out the cape's true nature.

The Mold Gold Cape was created from a single piece of gold about the size of a table tennis ball, beaten into an astonishingly thin and intricate form. The design imitates small beads, strung in layered strands, and this breathtaking piece of craftsmanship has yet to be paralleled by modern goldsmiths.

The cape is narrow across the shoulders and so could only have been worn by a very small adult, or perhaps more likely a child: slipped over the head and covering the upper part of the chest and shoulders like a poncho or shrug. Holes along the edges indicate that it was probably sewn onto a textile or leather base layer. Given its rigidity it's likely it was worn for special occasions. It was speculated that it may even have been created specifically for the burial, but micro-analysis of the surface indicates it has been handled repeatedly.

Nothing like this cape has ever been found before or since. It could be Welsh or Irish, or made from gold amassed from many different sources. Intriguingly, the findspot is near the route to the Great Orme copper mines in North Wales. This was a place of central importance in the Bronze Age, as copper is an essential component of bronze. To make bronze, you need copper and tin, but these ores never occur in the same place geologically, so bronze-making needs trade to exist. Coin-based money systems didn't exist in Britain at this time, so the copper would have been exchanged for other desirable resources and artefacts – cloth, meat, salt, perhaps slaves, and precious metals like gold. The people controlling the production and trade of copper from Great Orme would have been hugely powerful and wealthy.

So maybe this gold-clad child was linked to the leaders and traders of metal? Maybe they were young but already a leader in their own right? Or perhaps they were a sacred figure in the community – some kind of spiritual representative or priest, with a specific, sacred, role to play. We don't know why this cape is the only one we have. Maybe there is another one out there, waiting to be found.

Right The cape is solid and was beaten out of a single piece of gold about the size of a table tennis ball. It would fit a child.

Lindow Man Bog Body

A human sacrifice preserved in peat?

Cheshire

Left Stained orange by the natural tannin in the peat bog, Lindow Man's body is so perfectly preserved we can still appreciate his haircut and manicure, 2,000 years on.

At first the peat workers thought it was a piece of wood; then they realised it had toenails. They had found another Iron Age bog body: leathered, orange with tannin and astonishingly whole, given that the Lindow Man died 2,000 years ago.

The previous year a different human body part had been retrieved from Lindow Moss and, thinking he'd been found out, a local man confessed to killing his wife. But it turned out that this, too, was an ancient corpse. These bodies had been naturally preserved in the acidic, anaerobic (oxygen-free) conditions, which prevent bacterial breakdown. The level of preservation is so good that we can tell that the Lindow Man was in his twenties, his fingernails were manicured, and he kept his hair and beard neatly trimmed. His last meal – some unleavened wheat and barley bread – was still inside his preserved stomach.

We also know some of the details of his death. The young man was hit on the back of the head, and in the back, possibly with an axe. A thin cord was tied around his neck and he was garrotted, then his throat was cut from ear to ear. Finally, he was placed face down in a pool in the bog. CT scans have shown that his brain swelled before he died, so it's likely that he lay fatally injured for some hours before he took his final breath.

Was he a traveller set upon by murderous thieves? Was he publicly executed? Or could he be a human sacrifice? Bog bodies are found across northern Europe, in the liminal edgelands where water and earth meet. Three other ancient people have been found in Lindow Moss, and hundreds more have been unearthed in Ireland, Germany, Denmark and the Netherlands, mostly dating from around 700 BC–AD 200. Alongside them were deposits of weapons, tools and cauldrons: valuable items intentionally cast beyond everyday use.

The Lindow Man's manicure and smart hairdo suggests he enjoyed high status in life, and so could have been a valuable 'offering'. Or perhaps custom dictated that if something went wrong (a failed harvest, or a defeat in battle) then your leader – the king, or maybe his heir – would sacrifice himself. If you thought that your death might ensure the survival of your whole community, maybe you, too, would be willing to walk towards the water.

The big question is whether Lindow Man was placed into a bog because the Iron Age people of Lindow knew it had preservative properties. If he was an offering or messenger to the gods, then maybe there was sacred value in his body surviving beyond what would be normal for a corpse? But how would they know, unless they dug him up to check on his condition? It puts the mummified remains of Cladh Hallan (page 229), and the decomposed 'deviant' burials like the Childrey Warren woman (page 129) into an intriguing context. Lindow Man might spill more of his secrets as archaeological science advances, but for now his leathery lips are sealed.

Staffordshire Hoard

A treasure hoard from ancient Mercia

Staffordshire

Right The largest hoard of Anglo-Saxon gold ever found was unearthed from a farmer's field by a metal detectorist in 2009. Almost 6 kg (13 lb 4 oz) of gold, garnet and silver fragments were buried near to the Watling Street highway, within the kingdom of Mercia, in the late 600s AD. It's intriguing: there's only one complete item amongst the 4,600 fragments, a jewelled Christian cross. Every other piece of treasure was torn or cut from its 'parent object' before being buried. There are decorative fittings from more than a hundred weapons, mostly swords, but none of the blades. There are no items traditionally owned by women, no everyday objects, no dress fittings like belt buckles, and no coins. It suggests that this wasn't just general war booty, but a carefully curated collection, gathered over time. We don't know why this hoard was buried – Was it stolen? Is it a sacrifice? – but it would have been as rich and important to the hiders as it is to us.

Gosforth Cross

A towering vision of Viking Christianity

Cumbria

Left **The Viking cross in St Mary's churchyard.**

The Gosforth Cross is a remarkable piece of sandstone, 4.5 m (15 ft) high and precariously slim. It was carved in the early 900s AD, and although more than a thousand years of Cumbrian rain has erased some of the detail, it remains one of the most compelling and mysterious pieces of carved stone in Britain.

The lower portion of the shaft is round, then it squares off. Every surface on the upper portion is covered with elaborate Norse carvings – interlocking knotwork, fantastical horses and wolf- and dragon-headed creatures. There are images of Norse gods like Thor, Odin and Heimdallr . . . and yet, this is a Christian cross. The gods had been part of Norse people's spiritual and everyday life for centuries. Thor's hammer was what made thunder, the ravens in the trees were Odin's messengers, life itself was in the hands of the Norns (see Saltfleetby Spindle Whorl, page 63). So is it possible the makers of the Gosforth Cross carved these familiar characters simply as decoration, or a good set of stories? How do we otherwise explain this bizarre religious hybrid?

The Viking settlers in this part of Britain are hard to trace archaeologically. It appears that they arrived in the early 900s from either the Irish-Norse community, the Western Isles and Galloway or directly from Scandinavia, and took over fertile farmland on Britain's north-west coast. Whether the incomers integrated with the local Anglian and Celtic Cumbrians or totally displaced them, is unknown. What does seem clear, however, is that once the Norsemen did settle, they converted to Christianity quite quickly, and at least some of them were wealthy enough to start commissioning beautiful work like the Gosforth Cross. The way history is recounted often makes the past appear black-and-white. But the realities of faith might have been a little more grey.

The Gosforth carvings are carefully and intentionally ambiguous. On the western side, Loki, the trickster god, is shown enduring the punishment of the other gods. He's bound to three great stones by his own son's entrails, and poison drips into his eyes. He'll remain there until the end of time. It's a

Above Christ on the cross, attended by two female figures, surrounded by intricate knotwork and animals. Is the figure on the right a Valkyrie?
Right Ambiguous and beautiful. Trickster God Loki is punished until the end of time – could this also represent a sinner punished in Christian Hell?

Viking tale, but perhaps not incompatible with biblical passages describing the Devil bound, or the sinner punished in the bonds of Hell, awaiting Judgement Day. There are images of Heimdallr, the watchman, sounding the horn to mark the coming of the end of days, and Fenrir, the great wolf, killing Odin by swallowing him. The decision to show these characters in these particular stories is an interesting one; these are revered tales, but they also depict the death of the gods – and therefore, perhaps, the end of the Old Ways?

On the eastern side is an even more intriguing figure. It's most commonly interpreted as the crucifixion of Christ, and the only obviously Christian image. There's a figure of a man, arms outstretched, wearing a loincloth, with two figures below, looking up at him. The image is familiar from the canon of western Christian art. And yet all is not what it seems. The woman below has distinctively plaited hair, wears a trailing dress and is holding a horn. A Norse reading of the Virgin Mary? Or perhaps a valkyrie welcoming Jesus to Valhalla, the glorious otherworldly hall presided over by Odin?

The shape of the cross itself offers another theological connection – the rounded lower portion, reminiscent of a tree, probably represents the legendary ash tree Yggdrasil, which connects all the worlds at the centre of the Viking universe. But above that, the tree is tamed into a geometric pillar with flat edges. And at the top, surmounting all, are four 'triquetra', or trinity-knot symbols. They have their roots in European pagan traditions, but are best known as a symbol of the Christian Trinity of God, Jesus and the Holy Spirit.

The Gosforth Cross is profoundly original. It's an artistic masterpiece, and prompts a theological conversation that still engages us today. Are the Viking gods now harmless images, stripped of faith associations but retained for their cultural familiarity? Are these old, yet still powerful, stories co-opted to explain Christian messages? Or do they represent the conflict of new versus ancient faith, of leaders who have converted to the religion but whose followers (and perhaps even the stonemason) remain committed to the old gods? Humans have an extraordinary ability to hold conflicting beliefs, and to deploy different logic in different circumstances. But if you can find parallels between what you're teaching and what everyone already believes, you'll find a far more receptive audience.

The cross stands in the graveyard of St Mary's Church. Inside the church are two 'hogback' gravestones, a distinctly British Viking style of burial monument. They're probably the gravestones of local Viking chiefs, buried in the Christian tradition. We don't know if these individuals were the ones who commissioned the cross, and how much religious conflict they had to manage in their community. What's clear is that they were able to establish and sustain a community of craftspeople and masons who were able to execute rich and complex work. For many years, the Norse communities living in the north west of England have been written off as isolated farmers, just getting on with life. The Gosforth Cross demands we reappraise their cultural legacy.

Vale of York Viking Hoard

Worldly treasures buried in haste

North Yorkshire

Left This intricate silver cup discovered in a farmer's field was initially mistaken for a toilet ball-cock. It's actually solid silver, gilded with pure gold and inspired by Persian textile design. It dates to the mid-800s AD.

This extraordinary find was metal detected from a ploughed field near Harrogate, North Yorkshire. The two detectorists thought they'd found an old toilet ballcock, but then they realised that they'd unearthed a round cup, full of metal. Spilling out of the top were ancient coins, including a Saxon silver penny. They immediately realised they'd found treasure and alerted the authorities. The cup was taken to the British Museum and forensically excavated in 1 cm (²⁄₅ in) layers. The process took a whole, painstaking week.

The Vale of York Hoard comprises more than sixty pieces of silver including arm rings, ingots and jewellery fragments, a gold arm ring, 617 silver coins, bits of lead that once formed a makeshift cover on the top of the cup, and the cup itself – made of solid silver, exquisitely decorated and gilded with pure gold. The coins and jewellery came from all over the world, from Ireland to the Middle East, and based on the dates of the coins, the cup and its contents must have been buried in around AD 928 (the same generation that someone was carving the Gosforth Cross, page 207). In perfect and compact form this find represents the people of tenth-century Yorkshire and their dynamic global networks of trade and power.

The cup is a treasure of the medieval world. It's 9.2 cm (3²⁄₃ in) high and decorated with six 'roundel' designs, each containing a beautifully imagined animal – a lion, a wild cat, a deer, a stag, an antelope and a wild horse – surrounded by intricate leaf designs. The predators are springing forwards towards the prey animals; the beasts of the chase are fleeing wildly. The animal forms are more commonly seen on fine textiles from Persia, and the leaf designs are Frankish in style, from artists based in the powerful empire that is now modern-day France and western Germany. Based on the decorative schemes, art experts have been able to date the cup to the mid-800s AD, which means that by the time it was buried, it was more than one hundred years old. It's possible that it was originally created to hold consecrated bread in Christian mass. If so, it would have originally had a lid, and been hugely precious to its owners in terms of its spiritual as well as monetary value. It probably came into the possession of the Viking residents of North Yorkshire through raiding and then trading. But if the Vikings had just wanted it for its metal value, it would have been melted down. Clearly they appreciated this cup for its beauty.

The silver pieces in the hoard are ingots, fragments of jewellery used as currency ('hack-silver') and arm and neck rings. There are several Anglo-Scandinavian coins, probably minted in York. They bear the name St Peter, the patron saint of York, and incorporate the hammer of the Norse god Thor as the final 'I' in Petri ('Peter'). There are also four Frankish deniers and fifteen Islamic dirhams from the Middle East and Afghanistan. Most of the 617 coins in the hoard, however, are Anglo-Saxon silver pennies minted by Alfred the Great (r. 871–899), his son Edward the Elder (r. 899–924) and his grandson Athelstan (r. 924–939).

One single coin in the hoard declares Athelstan as 'King of All Britain' (REX TOTIUS BRITANNIAE) and was struck in late 927 or 928. This is the only coin of its type, and it doesn't look worn – so it seems likely this coin was new when it was buried. That might tell us a lot. This was the moment the Anglo-Saxon King Athelstan conquered Northumbria and created a single Kingdom of the 'English' for the first time in our island's history.

Vikings had raided Britain's coastal monasteries and communities since the 790s AD, but usually returned to Scandinavia with their loot and slaves. But in AD 865 a coalition force of Norwegian and Danish warriors, the Great Heathen Army, arrived to conquer. And they did – throughout the 860s AD, the Northmen extended their territories from East Anglia to Northumbria. Local communities were sometimes killed, sometimes displaced and sometimes integrated with the new settlers – we can see their legacy in place names and in people's DNA (the so-called 'Viking genes'). In AD 878 King Alfred of Wessex – later dubbed Alfred the Great – won a decisive battle against the Vikings, and forced them to divide the land. Alfred kept the south and west, and 'Danelaw' was established in the north and east.

But the royals of Wessex were expansionists and Alfred's son and grandson waged war with the aim of creating a single kingdom of the English, under the rule of one king. Athelstan forced submission from Cornwall, Wales and the Scots in quick succession, and took the Kingdom of Northumbria in AD 927. In York he declared himself 'King of All Britain'. His rule didn't last, but it was long enough for him to mint coins to mark his triumph. It's easy to tell this kind of tale in vast sweeps, where dynasties rise and fall and history marches inexorably on. But the reality behind the textbook blurb is that ordinary people's lives were shattered. In the wreckage some saw opportunity, perhaps many more saw great misery.

It seems most likely that someone buried this wealth in the Vale of York for safekeeping, perhaps in the aftermath of Athelstan's conquest, with running skirmishes, roving bands of soldiers and the threat of having to flee – or fight – for your life. It might have been loot that raiders planned to return for, or perhaps a family's hastily assembled valuables buried in a moment of terror. Excavation has failed to find any evidence of buildings or other activity in the area, so it seems that this was an anonymous field a thousand years ago, just as it is today.

The question remains: why didn't the people who buried this treasure come back to retrieve it? The hiding place may have been lost or forgotten. Perhaps the person planning to retrieve it fled the area and wasn't able to return. Or perhaps they were killed. This cup of treasures tells a big history of Vikings, Anglo-Saxons, invasion and defeat. But it also hints at a very human misadventure.

Below More than sixty pieces of silver and gold including arm rings, ingots, jewellery fragments and 617 silver coins, some from as far away as Afghanistan: this treasure represents the wealth and connectedness of the early medieval world.

Sunkenkirk

*A remote circle of
Neolithic ritual*

Cumbria

Right Also known as Swinside
Stone Circle, these fifty-five
stones nestle close to one
another and would have originally
formed a complete wall, save for
an entranceway on the south-
eastern side, flanked by two
portal, or gateway stones. This
is one of three significant stone
circles in Cumbria, together with
Long Meg and Her Daughters
near Penrith and Castlerigg
near Keswick, and they may
all be linked: they're some of
Britain's earliest stone circles,
central places for people to
gather, exchange precious goods,
and perform important social
rituals. Whether these were
sombre gatherings, or more like
parties involving hooking up and
getting high, isn't clear from the
archaeology.

Whithorn Eaves-Drip Burials

Baby burials in the shadow of the church

Dumfries

Left Archaeologists noted a strange phenomenon in a number of Anglo-Saxon burial grounds dating from the seventh to the eleventh centuries, including near Whithorn Priory in Scotland: the careful burial of babies and young children close to the walls of church buildings and churchyard boundaries. The graves cluster in the area where the rain would drip off the roof on to the ground below – hence, 'eaves-drip' burials. These might be unbaptized babies, buried unofficially. Only baptised individuals were entitled to burial in consecrated ground: children who died before christening would therefore be unable to enter Heaven. Perhaps local clergymen looked the other way when bereaved parents brought these tiny bundles for secret burial close to the mother church. Maybe the mourners hoped their little ones might be blessed by the raindrops, sanctified as they rolled off the church. Intriguingly, it appears that British Romans also buried their babies close to buildings, so it's possible eaves-drip burials are the Christianisation of a very ancient tradition.

Kilmartin Glen

Britain's Valley of the Kings

Argyll

Left The oldest surviving monument in Kilmartin Glen is the chambered tomb of Nether Largie South, built around 5,600 years ago. You can still enter this mysterious tomb. The outside was remodelled more than 1,000 years later to make it look more like the other burial cairns in the valley.

Next page Ballymeanoch is a curious collection of stone rows and other monuments that form yet another ritual alignment in Kilmartin Glen. They date from 2200–1200 BC, and incorporate stones that were decorated with prehistoric rock art carved more than 1,500 years earlier. The southerly stone row aligns with the Midsummer full moonrise. The northerly stone row aligns with the Midwinter sunrise.

An hour south of Oban, there's a valley chock full of astonishing prehistoric monuments, some almost 6,000 years old. And yet most people have never heard of it. If you visit Glebe Cairn, Nether Largie, Ri Cruin or Temple Wood, you'll be transported to an ancestral landscape of profound complexity, a Scottish version of the Valley of the Kings. Burial cairns and ritual sites run the full length of the valley, a dramatic statement of authority, ambition and perhaps sacred magic.

One of the first monuments to be built is one of the most enigmatic. On a natural gravel terrace at Upper Largie, two parallel lines of massive timber posts were erected, running for an astonishing 400 m (1,300 ft). Archaeologists call these long linear features 'cursus' monuments, but we have no idea what they are. Suggestions range from a race track, to a ceremonial pathway, to a spiritual 'no man's land' between spirit country and everyday space. The Kilmartin cursus burned down some time between 3800–3650 BC. It's unlikely to have been an accident, which means this was a destructive, transformative ritual act of gigantic proportions. A short time after the burning, the earliest burial chamber was constructed at Nether Largie South, around 3600 BC. It was designed to be able to be entered again and again, and you can still enter it now. It's a monument built by people who wanted an active relationship with the remains of their dead (just like at Isbister tomb, page 25). Perhaps bones and body parts were handled, arranged and taken in and out of the tomb, and living people would enter the tomb to commune with the ancestors.

As well as elaborate death and fire rites, the people of Kilmartin also troubled themselves with the heavens. The Temple Wood stone circles are some of the earliest ever constructed in Britain, and they started off, at least in part, as instruments for astronomical observations. First built in timber, they were checked and augmented, and about 100 years later, set in stone. The sites continued to be used for about 2,000 years,

Above The inside of Nether Largie South tomb is divided by low, vertically set stones, similar in style to Isbister on Orkney, some 400 miles away (page 25). We don't know what roles these different compartments played.

and were eventually modified to become burial monuments. Cairns were built next to the circles, and later, the circles themselves were turned into cairns. A Victorian landowner planted a stand of trees around the circles, and named the site Temple Wood. But even without the romantic name, this is a magical site; a place that seems to hold the memory of sacred acts performed.

The northernmost burial mound is Glebe Cairn, a vast heap of stones from the early Bronze Age (about 2200–1950 BC) that was built on top of two stone-lined boxes known as cists (the Gaelic word for 'chest', pronounced 'kiss-t'). The first was a cist made from stone slabs, which once contained a body. The body had totally disintegrated, but a pottery food bowl of a distinctive type from Ireland, and a necklace made from jet beads was found *in situ*. The second cist was made from boulders, and also originally held a person's body and an Irish style food vessel. We can only guess at the religious beliefs that would inform a burial rite like this, but it seems that maybe the dead were thought to go on a journey and they would need to eat, or give food as an offering to some entity beyond the grave. Not everyone would have received this kind of burial – or had the status to own as rare and exquisite a treasure as the jet necklace. Jet isn't actually stone, it's semi-fossilized wood, which gives it strange and magical properties – it floats, it can burn and it can give you an electric shock. It's also not native to Kilmartin – the closest extraction site is 480 km (300 miles) away in Whitby, Yorkshire. How did the jet necklace reach the west of Scotland? This was a time before money, so it would have been traded for goods, or given as a gift, perhaps in a long chain of exchanges between important people. It may have also come with someone who travelled here from Yorkshire – even in prehistoric times, people were mobile and adventurous!

Ri Cruin is the southernmost burial site, restored to its original 20-m (65-ft) diameter, with three cists within. We're not sure who the people in any of these cists were, but they were clearly high status. Many of the stones in the cists were carved with images of bronze axeheads. Elsewhere in Britain axehead markings are rare (Stonehenge being a notable exception), but in Kilmartin Glen they appear again and again. Seven axehead carvings are still visible on the inside of the end slab of the cist on the western side of Ri Cruin. What did the axeheads represent? Did they say something about the person within, their family or loyalties, or did they speak to the gods or ancestors? These symbols might also represent the source of these people's prestige, and the reason why they were motivated to construct such a vast monumental landscape.

Kilmartin Glen is strategically important. It's the route to the sea and therefore trade with the continent and Ireland. It's the link to people in western Scotland and further inland. If the Kilmartin elites were in control of the raw materials to make bronze – tin and copper – as well as access to the metalworking experts, they would have been unassailable. But towards the end of the Bronze Age the weather turned colder and wetter and peat began to form on the farmland around Kilmartin. Trade networks shifted, and ultimately, iron smelting developed elsewhere and trumped bronze working entirely. The glory days of Kilmartin Glen and its powerful rulers were over.

The dramatic fortress of Dunadd, the royal seat of the Gaelic Kings from around AD 600–900, lies just 6 km (3¾ miles) south (page 225). It's entirely possible that one of the reasons it rose to become the foremost royal site, and the place of royal inauguration, was because of its proximity to the ancient monuments of Kilmartin. At Dunadd, men were transformed into monarchs – perhaps they absorbed some of the authority of those most ancient ancestors, still watching from their rock-girt tombs further up the glen.

Below The central grave (cist) and surrounding cairn within Temple Wood southern circle. The outer circle was first designed in timber, adjusted and then rebuilt in stone.

Dunadd

Fortress of the Gaelic warriors

Argyll

Left The dramatic entranceway to Dunadd fortress, hewn through the natural rock terraces.

Dunadd is immediately arresting. A rocky crag rising dramatically out of the low fields, it's a striking sight, even now. 1,300 years ago it was where kings were made.

First fortified in the Iron Age, Dunadd ultimately became the Royal Fortress at the centre of the Kingdom of Dál Riata, the land of the Gaels. These people were also known as the Scotti, which originated as a Latin term used by the Romans to describe Gaelic sea raiders. Scotti is a derogatory term, probably meaning 'pirates' and it's where we get the modern name 'Scotland' from. At its peak, the Gaelic warrior kings ruled territory spanning Northern Ireland and western Scotland. Their domination did not mean peace: there was infighting between the Gaelic families, battles with the Picts to the north-east, the Angles and Britons to the east and south and, from the late 700s onwards, with 'Northmen' from Scandinavia. Dunadd was naturally defensible, visually impressive, and well located above the River Add (Dun-Add means 'Fortified Hill on the Add'): a gateway between Scotland and the sea.

Compared to elite palaces in other regions, Gaelic royal fortress sites are often small. Given that rulers could requisition any land they liked, it seems certain that 'bijou' was a deliberate preference. Certainly what Dunadd lacks in floor space, it makes up for in dramatic elevation. The buildings were timber-framed with thatched roofs, possibly brightly painted and boasting carved decoration. There would have been houses, workshops and a hall for feasting and gathering. Surrounding them were circuits of defences, some hand-cut, others utilising the natural rock crags.

The regular folk farmed the surrounding landscape. They raised sheep, pigs and cattle, grew oats and barley, and fished and hunted. But they, too, were part of the hierarchical and war-hungry society; households were expected to provide tribute to the rulers, and when war bands were drafted, young men and battle-hardened veterans would be drawn from

225

Above Towering over a modern farm, the fortress rises up from the flat land of the Mòine Mhòr, the Great Moss and the River Add valley.

every home. Success meant wealth and the patronage of the king. Failure would mean slavery at the hands of the enemy, or death.

Between the fighting, the Dál Riatan elite lived a fine life. The remains of spice jars, glass and wine vessels at Dunadd suggest trade links to the Mediterranean and western Europe. French pottery has been found containing traces of madder dye which produces a rich blood-red cloth. There's evidence of gold, silver, bronze and iron-working here, too. The craftspeople, under the king's patronage, would have made tools and weapons, but also jewellery, especially brooches; these were given as gifts from the king to those who pledged their fealty. The brooches themselves are rare survivors, but on Dunadd, excavators have found hundreds of fragments of clay moulds used to form molten metal into the Celtic knots, bird-head designs and other elaborate pieces that would have been pinned on to diplomats and warriors.

Dunadd was a place of religious power too. Although we don't have written documents from Dál Riata, the leaders were probably literate, and hosted monks and priests from the nearby holy island of Iona, one of the most powerful Christian sites in Europe.

The relationship between warrior king and the peace-teaching early Church is perhaps surprising to us now, but it was mutually beneficial. The king could provide protection and resources, while the monks could educate the sons of elite families, make diplomatic visits to neighbouring kingdoms, and demonstrate their blessing – and therefore approval – of the king's authority. It's no coincidence that Dunadd is surrounded by place names with the component 'kil', which means church or chapel.

Dunadd wasn't just a place for kings to live; it was also a place where kings were made. In every generation, a king would be selected from the elite, royal families. Your suitability for the role was based not just on your lineage, but also your strength as a warrior, and your diplomatic ability, an absolute necessity in order to manage a complex war-mongering maritime nation.

The inauguration of a king was both spiritual and physical, a moment which forged an unbreakable relationship between the king, the land and the people. One of the most extraordinary elements of this powerful place are the carvings in the rock used in the inauguration ceremonies of the kings – a footprint, a carving of a boar, an illegible line of ogham inscription and a carved circular hole possibly used as a ritual basin. They've been assailed by centuries of brutal wind and rain, but they're still visible.

The details of the inauguration ceremonies have been lost, but it's thought that the would-be king placed his foot inside the footprint in the rock (modern UK shoe size 6; US size 8). In that act, he would be bonded absolutely with the land and the people. The ceremony probably fused the traditions of Christian ordination and pagan kingship, appealing to both the old power systems and the new.

In AD 736 the Picts (page 39) seized Dunadd, and the Gaelic elites were forced to submit to their rule. From the 790s, life was further disrupted by Viking raids. The Picts and the Gaels were eventually united under the kingship of Cináed mac Alpín (Kenneth MacAlpin) in AD 842 and the rulers that followed. The seat of power in this new territory, Alba, shifted east to Forteviot near Perth. Dunadd remained occupied, but it was no longer the stronghold that created kings.

The power of the rock has faded, but its magic remains. Climb up through the dramatic gap in the rock terrace that formed the kings' entrance and scramble over more lines of defences to the top of the citadel. The real footprint is now hidden beneath a protective replica, but it's identical. Place your foot inside the shape, just like the ancient kings of Dál Riata, and take in the commanding view across their once-mighty kingdom.

Below Climb to the summit and place your foot in the mystical footprint used by Gaelic warrior kings some 1,300 years ago.

Cladh Hallan Mummies

Mummification in the Bronze Age

South Uist, Outer Hebrides

Left The low remains of prehistoric roundhouses at Cladh Hallan.

On the Scottish island of South Uist, a row of Bronze Age roundhouses dating to around 1200 BC were home to a village of farmers and fisherfolk. The front doors faced east, cooking and craft remains were consistently in the southern sections of the houses and sleeping areas in the northern sections. When archaeologists excavated beneath the floor of the central house, they found the body of a young teenage girl. Under the southern house, there was the body of a three-year-old child. Under the northern house, there were the bodies of a man on the north side and a woman on the south side.

The adults appear to have been tightly wrapped in crouched positions, like Peruvian mummy bundles. You can't make a fresh human body bend as tightly as these people are folded, with spines, shinbones and thigh bones almost parallel to one another. It's clear the flesh had dried out while the bones stayed in position, held together by preserved tissues like tendons and ligaments. Their bones also show that the normal bacterial activity you'd expect to find in a dead body suddenly stopped. How does this happen in the damp climate of South Uist, which would otherwise be perfect for decomposing corpses? The intriguing explanation is that these Bronze Age farmers were practising ritual mummification.

Analysis of the Cladh Hallan bones reveals they've been stained by tannin, and exposed to an acidic environment that would have helped preserve the whole corpse. The most likely candidate for such a site is the nearby peat bog. But unlike bog bodies that were placed in the bog and never retrieved (see Lindow Man, page 203), these bodies were put in for long enough to 'cure' them, probably a few months, then brought out again, dried and maintained.

The bodies, however, are even more bizarre than they first seem. Radiocarbon dating shows the Cladh Hallan woman and man had been dead for as many as 300 years before they were buried beneath the house. And DNA analysis reveals that they're not actually, simply, a woman and a man at all – they're composites made from at least three people's bodies. The woman's right upper arm, right thigh bone and right jawbone were all from different people. Before she was buried, they snapped off her knee and buried it in a separate pit. Her wrist was also broken off and placed near a pit containing a number of cremations. Finally, her attendants carefully removed her two front teeth and put them into her mummified hands – left tooth in her left hand, right tooth in her right hand.

The male body under the northern house floor was also a jigsaw. Everything from the neck down was one man, a second man had provided the skull and neck vertebrae and a third, the jaw. With two composites, it seems less likely that this was a one-off, or an accident where people got jumbled up accidentally. Perhaps 'multi-mummies' could unite important families in the clan, or underpin peace treaties with former enemies.

Further analysis showed the child under the southern house was also mummified, although the position of the body meant that this was less apparent than with the adults. The proof was again in the lack of bacterial activity in the bones, which can only be seen under a microscope. It raises the intriguing possibility that there may be the skeletal remains of once-mummified people right across British Bronze Age sites that look like 'normal' burials. If we didn't know to look for evidence, it's no surprise we haven't found it.

In all the cultures of the world that practise mummification, we find people maintaining complex and active relationships with the bodies. Mummies are social and they act like people, often working as intermediaries between the spirits and the living, or offering protection or wisdom.

All the bodies at Cladh Hallan were buried as 'foundation deposits', while the houses were first being built. Some years later, when the central and northern houses underwent significant rebuilds, the residents buried more corpses – two dogs and a baby – and this time, they were fresh bodies. Perhaps these were additional offerings, or guardians. We don't know why these fresh bodies were buried alongside the mummies. Maybe they performed different roles, or maybe it was a pragmatic decision because there weren't enough mummies available. It's controversial, but we can't rule out the idea that the baby was sacrificed in order to be buried under the house.

Houses can be places of functional domesticity, but also places that are magical, powerful and full of spiritual importance. Modern Mongolian nomads arrange their circular yurts in distinct practical and spiritual ways: the entrance always faces south, the hearth is in the middle, and the most honoured spot on the north is for guests as well as sacred objects and spirit shrines. Men sit and work on the right (east), and women sit and work on the left (west). Young people are expected to stay by the door. Whenever you move around the house, you move 'sunwise' (clockwise), following the path of the sunlight on the floor of the yurt as the day progresses. The hearth is the centre of the home, the centre of the universe, and through the smoke rising upwards, it links the Earth to the upper realm of spirits and gods. The yurt becomes a microcosm of the universe.

Modern Mongolians and prehistoric Hebridean islanders don't share a religious worldview. But clearly in both cases, the home is much more than a place of everyday labour. In Cladh Hallan, the door was always in the east, working was done on one side and sleeping on the other. All the burials, except the woman, were in the houses' north-eastern quadrants. If you moved around a roundhouse in the same way you move around a yurt – sunwise – then the bodies would be between the sleeping area and the exit. Maybe that's the best description we have for the people under the floor: they were somewhere between sleep and the exit – part of daily life, but also beyond. They were neither alive nor dead, both at once.

Calanais

The Stonehenge you've never heard of

Isle of Lewis, Outer Hebrides

Left The 5 m (16 ft) central monolith at Calanais I has a distinctive angled top, and stands at the centre of a stone circle with lines of stones running to the cardinal points. A thousand years after the first stones were erected, a chamber was built at the centre of the circle, perhaps to hold human remains.

If this place were nearer London, there's little doubt that it would be world-famous, drawing tourists by the coachload. But it's not – it's on a windswept promontory on the Isle of Lewis, in the Outer Hebrides off Scotland's west coast. Calanais, also spelled Callanish, is a complex of monuments with this magnificent cross-shaped stone alignment, Calanais I, at its centre. It's a dramatic and wild place, and from most directions of approach, the stones stand silhouetted on the horizon. They terrify and compel in equal measure, and there's no doubting you're entering a place with great potency.

Calanais I comprises a 12 m (40 ft) wide circle made from thirteen irregular stones, a towering 5 m (16 ft) monolith at its centre (*mono-* meaning 'single'; *-lith* meaning 'stone') and lines of stones running to the cardinal points. An 83 m (272 ft) long avenue of paired stones runs north, and single lines of stones lead east, south and west. The stones are unworked blocks of the local Lewisian Gneiss, which is the oldest rock in Britain (a staggering 3 billion years old, two-thirds the age of the planet). They're a rich, swirling grey, stone giants standing tall against the wind.

Radiocarbon dating has revealed that the circle, central pillar and southern line were all erected between 2900–2600 BC, making this monument slightly older than the sarsen stone arrangements at Stonehenge (page 115). After a thousand years of use, the north, east and west lines were added, and rather unusually, a chambered cairn, or some kind of bone crypt, was built inside the circle with an entrance facing east. These stones are the centrepiece of a vast ritual landscape. The surrounding moorland boasts at least eleven stone circles, nine stone rows, single standing stones and burial cairns.

As always with these stone monuments, we wonder what they were for and how they were used. The evidence points to Calanais I being designed as an astronomical observatory, perhaps related to the movements of the moon. One of the most compelling alignments is that if you're standing in the circle on the night the moon is at the extreme lowest point in the sky – every 18.6 years – it perfectly skims the southern hills on the horizon. While it sounds a little far-fetched that farmers living 5,000 years ago might have noticed an evening of perfect moonshine every two decades or so, especially in a place that has a fair few cloudy nights, other ancient sources indicate people did exactly that. In Greek documents, the Hyperboreans are described as a race of distant people who live on an ocean island beyond the north wind. Diodorus of Sicily says, 'the moon, as viewed from this island, appears to be but a little distance from the Earth . . . the moon god visits the island every nineteen years'. The poet Hecataeus of Abdera wrote that the Hyperboreans lived 'beyond the land of the Celts', with a 'magnificent sacred precinct of Apollo . . . spherical in shape'. Even when we allow for storytellers' elaborations, the initial similarities are intriguing.

Recent work at the site has also identified stones in the circle that align with Midsummer sunrise, and that the small group of stones around the natural hillock next to the main circle, Cnoc an Tursa ('Hill of Sorrows' in Gaelic), can function as a sundial. The group forms a rough cave shape, and archaeologists working at the site noticed that around midday on sunny days, a narrow shaft of sunlight shone between the stones from the back of the 'cave' onto the turf in front. This grassy forecourt area has been noted for its complex archaeological remains of posts, pits and ditches. The current theory supposes that this feature could have been used as a clock, and with additional markers or posts could also distinguish the solar year and divide

it into months. We don't know how the people here divided and measured time, but this offers intriguing possibilities.

Careful archaeological research is building a biography of Calanais. The original stones were erected on land that had been cultivated, but once monumental construction really got going, 'normal' life might have moved a little further away. The monument seems to have fallen out of favour some time between 1500–1000 BC and people returned to living nearby, and possibly even reused the chambered cairn in the centre of the circle for domestic use as a shelter or store. At least one pile of stones previously interpreted as a sacred burial cairn is probably the remains of a corn-drying kiln. It's a useful lesson to be watchful for turning every old lump or bump into 'ritual'. But even if you discard half the evidence at Calanais, you're left with an incontrovertible truth: this place was special.

For the people of late Neolithic Britain, Calanais may have been as famous as Stonehenge is today. Visitors might have travelled hundreds of miles to see it, or perhaps whispered about a mystical semi-legendary place that normal folk weren't allowed to approach. If Calanais was the Great Observatory in the North, where the people could claim direct knowledge of the movements of the gods in the heavens, they may have been considered to be almost divine themselves. In a world reliant on kind summers and good harvests, measured by the rising and setting of the sun, moon and stars, and controlled by the gods – what power that must have been.

Index

Page numbers in *italics* refer to captions

Further reading

Aldhouse-Green, Miranda. *The Celtic Myths: A Guide to the Ancient Gods and Legends*, Thames & Hudson, London, 2015.

Burnham, Andy (ed.). *The Old Stones: A Field Guide to the Megalithic Sites of Britain and Ireland*, Watkins Publishing, London, 2018.

Ochota, Mary-Ann. *Hidden Histories: A Spotter's Guide to the British Landscape*, Frances Lincoln, London, 2016.

Oliver, Neil. *The Story of the British Isles in 100 Places*, Bantam Press, London, 2018.

Pryor, Francis. *The Making of the British Landscape*, Allen Lane, London, 2010.

To explore 1.5 million archaeological finds made by members of the public in England and Wales, head to the Portable Antiquities Scheme database at www.finds.org.uk. To digitally wander around old maps, head to maps.nls.uk, run by the National Library of Scotland. The nations each have online resources with valuable records of their ancient sites: Wales: www.coflein.gov.uk; Scotland: www.canmore.org.uk; England: www.heritagegateway.org.uk.

Picture credits

Acknowledgments

Over the course of many years I've had the extraordinary privilege of meeting, talking to and working with some of the most talented archaeological researchers and scholars in the country. Sometimes it's at an event, sometimes it's on Twitter, sometimes it's in a muddy field or drafty cloister with a TV crew in tow. They've told me fascinating things on camera and also while we're waiting for the next take. They've let me rootle in stores and wander across sites. They've helped reveal some of the strangest details and what-else-could-it-be theories.

Particular thanks to the following people for advising on sites and finds in this book, or kindly reading half-baked drafts. Needless to say, all the errors – and a few of the crackpot theories – are my own.

Prof. Miranda Aldhouse-Green at the University of Cardiff; Dr Hugo Anderson-Whymark at the National Museum of Scotland; Dr Janet Bell at Glastonbury Abbey; Dr Tom Booth at the Natural History Museum; Dr Lee Bray at the Dartmoor National Park; Dr Alison Brookes at Corinium Museum; Dr Hannah Burrows at the University of Aberdeen; Dr Sharon Clough and Dr Alistair Barclay at Cotswold Archaeology; Glynn Davis at Colchester Museums; Prof. Ronald Hutton at the University of Bristol; Dr Nigel Jeffries at MOLA; Dr Jim Leary at the University of York; Prof. Michael Lewis and the team of dedicated finds liaison officers and specialists who run the Portable Antiquities Scheme (www.finds.org.uk); Paul Mortimer, scholar of all things Raedwald; Prof. Gordon Noble at the University of Aberdeen; Dr Richard Osgood, archaeologist at the Ministry of Defence; Nicky Paton, who looks after Royston Cave; Prof. Josh Pollard, at the University of Southampton; Andrew Price, Welsh hill wanderer who's found ringing stones and ancient caves with me; Dr Win Scutt at English Heritage; Dr Dave Stewart who re-wrote the book on Isbister; Dr Antonia Thomas at the University of the Highlands and Islands; Natalie Walker, who told me all about herballs; Dr Christie Willis, expert in all things Stonehenge; Dr Alex Woolf at the University of St Andrews.

Superhenge-sized thanks to Marianne Levy, who carved out infinitely better texts from rough hewn material; Merle Ochota for being a litmus on whether things were interesting; wild wanderers Miriam Craig and Anna Gorringe for climbing hills and holloways; top storyteller Jason Buck for tales that have fed my imagination and kept me gnawing on the meaty question of why; John Finnemore for drawing a wonderful wifey; my agents, Antony Topping at Greene and Heaton, and Helen Purvis and the team at Knight Ayton Management; the talented folk at Frances Lincoln, including editor Michael Brunström, publisher Philip Cooper and group publisher and general cheerleader Richard Green. And lastly but never leastly, Joe, Cole and Harpo, eternal sufferers of the stones.

Mary-Ann Ochota is a familiar face on TV archaeology programmes, including the cult show *Time Team*, History Channel's *Ancient Impossible*, BBC's *Britain Afloat* and the hit Smithsonian Channel show *Mystic Britain*.

She's written two other popular archaeology books, including *Hidden Histories: A Spotter's Guide to the British Landscape*, which was shortlisted for *Current Archaeology*'s Book of the Year Award. Mary-Ann also writes regularly for newspapers and magazines on outdoor adventures, anthropology and archaeology, presents documentaries on radio and podcasts, gives guided walks and performs archaeological storytelling. She's a Fellow of the Royal Geographical Society, a hillwalking ambassador for the British Mountaineering Council and she holds an MA from Cambridge University in Archaeology and Anthropology.

www.maryannochota.com
@maryannochota

Secret Britain
First published in 2020 by
Frances Lincoln Publishing,
an imprint of The Quarto Group,
The Old Brewery, 6 Blundell Street,
London N7 9BH, United Kingdom
T (0)20 7700 6700 F (0)20 7700 8066
www.QuartoKnows.com

Text copyright © Mary-Ann Ochota
Illustrations copyright © page 238

ISBN 978-0-7112-5346-9
10 9 8 7 6 5 4 3 2 1

Typeset in Swift and Whitney
Design by Glenn Howard
Printed in China

Brimming with creative inspiration, how-to projects and useful information to enrich your everyday life, Quarto Knows is a favourite destination for those pursuing their interests and passions. Visit our site and dig deeper with our books into your area of interest: Quarto Creates, Quarto Cooks, Quarto Homes, Quarto Lives, Quarto Drives, Quarto Explores, Quarto Gifts, or Quarto Kids.